Around the world in

80bites

Around the world in

80bites

Savor the aromas and flavors of 80 of the world's

greatest snacks, bites, mezze, and tapas!

Sunil Vijayakar

hamlyn

NOTES

The FDA advises that eggs should not be consumed raw. This book contains dishes made with raw or lightly cooked eggs. It is prudent for more vulnerable people such as pregnant and nursing mothers, invalids, the elderly, babies and young children to avoid uncooked or lightly cooked dishes made with eggs. Once prepared, these dishes should be kept refrigerated and used promptly.

Pepper should be freshly ground black pepper unless otherwise stated.

Fresh herbs should be used, unless otherwise stated.

Ovens should be preheated to the specified temperature—if using a fan-assisted oven, follow the manufacturer's instructions for adjusting the time and the temperature.

To Lou, Evan, Colin and Gregg.

First published in Great Britain in 2005 by
Hamlyn, a division of Octopus Publishing Group Ltd
2–4 Heron Quays, London E14 4JP

ISBN 0 600 61437 9
EAN 9780600614371

A CIP catalogue record for this book is available from the British Library

Printed and bound in China

10 9 8 7 6 5 4 3 2 1

CONTENTS

INTRODUCTION
6

EUROPE
12

AFRICA
56

ASIA
80

100
AUSTRALASIA

118
SOUTH AND
CENTRAL AMERICA

138
CARIBBEAN

158
NORTH AMERICA

GLOSSARY 186

INDEX 188

ACKNOWLEDGMENTS 192

INTRODUCTION

6 **The world on a plate**

The world is a fascinating place, not least because of the diversity of its countries and their respective cultures. And if there is one element of a country that typifies its cultural, historical, and social uniqueness more tellingly than any other, it has to be its food. At its most basic, food is essential for survival; however, it can also be a great pleasure. The cuisines of countries around the globe have developed as much in response to this secondary factor, as they have to the first. The social element of eating and drinking has brought families and friends together to celebrate, enemies together to negotiate, and leaders together to contemplate, since humans first roamed the planet. Sharing food is a bonding ritual that can overcome language barriers and cultural disparities; by sampling the typical food of a country or region you are at the same moment stepping back in time and immersing yourself in the history of that place. Knowledge of a country's cuisine is an essential part of the knowledge of the country itself, and the stories behind the recipes can be as interesting as the dishes themselves, with many steeped in ancient tradition.

Variations on a theme

The abundance of indigenous ingredients in certain countries resulted in the development of dishes to use them, but from meat through to breads and sauces, similar dishes are interpreted very differently, depending on the other ingredients available. Bread of some description is a staple food in many countries, yet there are significant variations in appearance, texture, and cooking techniques, depending on where you travel. Irish soda bread (Smoked Salmon and Gubbeen Bites, page 21) uses bicarbonate of soda as a leavening agent because the bread was first baked before yeast was widely used; German rye bread (Beefsteak Tartare on Endive Scoops variation, page 26) is made with rye flour rather than wheat; while the Mexican tortilla (Spinach and Bell Pepper Quesadillas, page 120) was traditionally made from corn, a predominant crop in that part of the world.

Trading tastes

Although individual ingredients in typical recipes are often native to the country, this is not always the case. Many well-

8 known dishes have resulted from trade, immigration, or exploration, with the introduction of new foods and cooking methods to a country that were subsequently adopted into its pantry. For example, the potato, unheard of in Europe until Sir Walter Raleigh brought some back from Virginia to Great Britain in the 1590s, was soon introduced into the repertoire of cooks around the continent and now features heavily in typical dishes of many European countries, particularly Ireland and England (Crispy Whitebait and French-fry Cones, page 25). Another example is the classic American hot dog (New York-style Hot Dogs, page 172)—German immigrants brought their taste for sausages with them to the USA in the early 1800s and began to sell them as a quick snack from carts on the street. The rest, as they say, is history!

Sugar and spice

The item that has probably had the greatest impact on cuisine around the world is sugar. First brought to England in the 14th century, sugar had by then already had a long history, having been imported from its native Pacific islands' home to India and other parts of Asia before reaching mainland Europe. As its popularity increased and sugar cane production expanded to cope with demand, there followed a tarnished period in sugar's history. Sugar cane was one of the crops that relied almost entirely on slave labor, and millions of Africans were forcibly removed from their homes or sold by local slave owners and transported to the new plantations in the Caribbean, in order to work for and line the pockets of European traders. As sugar became more widely available, its price dropped and it became a common foodstuff rather than the prized luxury of previous years.

Other ingredients that were rare and highly expensive when first introduced to the Western world were spices; although taken for granted these days, there was a time when peppercorns were counted out and sold individually. There was intense competition amongst many European countries for mastery of the spice trade and this required control over the spice-producing countries (this was the impetus for Christopher Columbus to set out on the voyage that led to the discovery of

America). Eventually England was established as the country in control of this precious trade, which brought with it substantial wealth and power. As with sugar, once spices became more readily available, they were used in a variety of recipes as a flavoring for meat, poultry, and desserts.

Growth of trade

An increase in trade between nations, and advances in transport, meant that food could be moved between countries quickly and effectively, while the introduction of exotic ingredients into mainstream European cooking resulted in an increased awareness and interest in food, as people sampled the cuisines of other countries for the first time. It seems strange to think that not long before 1600, no one outside the Americas had ever seen a tomato or potato, yet these were to become two of the basic staple foods in European cooking and were so successful because they flourished in the colder climate.

Despite the steadily increasing trade between Europe and the Americas, it was not just in Europe that new foods were introduced. As ships docked to fill the stores with exotic spices and seedlings, other products would be offloaded or traded, and produce and animals would find themselves in new homes. Early settlers in the Americas brought the seeds of favorite crops with them, while the slave trade also had a major impact on food and eating habits—transporting foods and seeds from West Africa to the Caribbean and the Americas, where crops, such as okra, were successfully cultivated and became an integral part of the emergent cuisine of those regions.

The great divide

Although many recipes are traditional throughout the length and breadth of a country, there are almost always regional specialties, again dependent on the ingredients specific to customs and cultural variations existing within different regions. In the days when transport was difficult or even nonexistent, people traveled very rarely and usually only out of necessity, and thus specialized dishes remained specific to their region. Cheese is one such product that remains highly regional, with independent cheese-makers maintaining age-old recipes and methods. Other examples include the pasta and risotto dishes of Italy, which vary greatly between the regions, or the vastly different cuisines of the United States. You'll find regional dishes or variations of national dishes in most countries and sampling them can be one of the most rewarding and memorable aspects of traveling in a foreign country.

Bite-size samples

As well as regional culinary variations, many countries have a strong tradition of street food, and in a book of bite-size portions it's worth mentioning this phenomenon. Essentially what is being created on the street is a miniature taster of some of the elements of a country's typical food—giving you an idea of the ingredients and cooking techniques that are used and the combinations of flavors that go into typical dishes of that country. From the hot dogs of New York to the samosas of India, street food is a split-second culinary tour that should not only appease hunger but rather assault all the senses at once—smell, taste, sight, touch, and hearing should all be treated to the experience. Food stalls are a place for people to gather, gossip, and grab a bite to eat. The food markets of countries such as Singapore and Thailand go one step further, since every conceivable local and national dish is on offer. At first the huge choice can be disconcerting, but it becomes immensely enjoyable once you've succumbed to the mouth-watering aromas and the constant barrage of noise. There is something very comforting about people meeting to eat and talk; it is perhaps why entertaining, more often than not, involves food. Spanish tapas and Greek mezze both work on the principle of little tasters of dishes—food that can be shared. The Swedish smörgåsbord is a similar concept and other variations exist around the world. Whether it's the way the bread is cooked, the way the meat is cured or the exact combination of spices or other flavors used, every recipe is unique and has evolved through many years of preparation, adaptation, and evolution. By sampling the dishes that follow, you will experience a taste of the cuisines of numerous countries around the world and a sense of the history behind their creation.

EUROPE

14 Herring and dilled-cucumber skewers

Using a vegetable peeler, cut the cucumber into long, thin slices and put them into a shallow, non-reactive bowl. Mix the vinegar with the sugar, stir in the dill and pour over the cucumber. Season well with salt and pepper, cover and allow to pickle in the refrigerator for 3–4 hours.

Meanwhile, make the dipping sauce. Finely grate the beet in a food processor or blender. Add the sour cream and mayonnaise and blend until fairly smooth and pink, then chill until ready to use.

To serve, thread a herring fillet onto a wooden or bamboo skewer with some of the cucumber slices. Repeat with the remaining herring and cucumber to give you 15 skewers. Serve at room temperature with the dipping sauce.

Makes 15

15 canned or bottled pickled herring (*matjes*) fillets, drained, or 15 rollmop herring fillets

Dilled cucumber
1 large cucumber
³⁄₄ cup white wine vinegar
2 teaspoons superfine sugar
3 tablespoons finely chopped dill
salt and pepper

Pink beet sour cream dipping sauce
1 small beet, about 2 oz, cooked and peeled
¹⁄₂ cup sour cream
¹⁄₂ cup mayonnaise

The **smörgåsbord** is Sweden's **most famous type** of cuisine, where many different foods are served, **buffet-style**, at the table. This recipe recreates the **tradition in miniature.**

Rye, chive, and cream cheese squares 17

Put the cream cheese and pickled cucumber into a small bowl and beat until smooth. Using a small spatula, spread the mixture thickly onto the rye bread squares.

Using a very sharp knife or a very sharp pair of kitchen scissors, very finely chop the chives and spread onto a plate in a thick, even layer. Working carefully and neatly, dip each bread square, cream cheese side down, into the chopped chives to coat it evenly with the chives. Put the bread, chive-side up, on a serving platter and arrange a slice of cucumber and red radish in the center of each square. Season well with salt and pepper, garnish with more chives if desired, and serve immediately.

Makes 20

1 cup cream cheese
1 tablespoon very finely diced pickled cucumber
20 squares of very dark rye bread, cut into 1½ inch squares
large bunch of chives
20 very thin slices of cucumber
20 very thin slices of red radish
salt and pepper
extra chives, to garnish

Smorrebrod are open sandwiches that are traditionally served at lunchtime in Danish cafés. These are a bite-size version.

18 Mini quail Scotch eggs

Put the eggs in a medium saucepan and cover with cold water. Bring to a boil, stirring gently to center the yolks, then simmer for 4–5 minutes. Drain the eggs, then put under cold running water. When cool, carefully remove the shells and set the eggs aside.

Put the ground chicken, mustard, mint jelly, and parsley in a bowl. Season with salt and pepper and mix well until thoroughly combined. Divide the mixture into 12 portions.

Toss the eggs in a little all-purpose flour and shake off the excess. Using lightly floured hands, shape a portion of chicken mixture around each egg to form a neat ball. Dip each ball into the beaten egg, then roll in the bread crumbs to coat evenly.

Pour the oil into a deep-fat fryer to a depth of at least 3 inches and heat to 350°F. Deep-fry the balls for 4–5 minutes until well browned, then drain on paper towels. When cool enough to handle, cut the balls in half and serve immediately or at room temperature.

Makes 24

12 quails' eggs
10 oz finely ground chicken
1 teaspoon English mustard
1 teaspoon mint jelly
2 tablespoons finely chopped parsley
all-purpose flour, for tossing
1 egg, lightly beaten
1⅓ cups natural dried bread crumbs
sunflower oil, for deep-frying
salt and pepper

These little bites are lighter than traditional Scotch eggs, the tiny quails' eggs being covered with ground chicken instead of sausagemeat.

Smoked Salmon and Gubbeen Bites   21

Using a 1 inch round biscuit or pastry cutter, stamp out 20 rounds from the soda bread. Mix the butter with the mustard and spread it thickly over the bread rounds.

Using the cutter, stamp out 20 rounds of the Gubbeen and use to top the prepared bread rounds, then use the cutter to stamp out 20 rounds of the smoked salmon and put those on top of the cheese.

To serve, put the soda bread canapés on a serving platter and squeeze a little lemon juice over each one. Season with the pepper and serve immediately.

Makes 20

8–9 thin slices of Irish soda bread
$\frac{1}{2}$ cup butter, softened
1 tablespoon wholegrain mustard
12 oz Irish Gubbeen cheese, thinly sliced
12 oz Irish smoked salmon, thickly sliced

To serve
lemon juice
pepper

A **pale cheese** with a **tough zest** and **crumbly texture,** **Gubbeen** is made from **cow's milk**. The name refers to a **bay** in **West Cork** where the cheese is produced.

22 Goats' cheese and red bell pepper puffs

Lightly grease a baking sheet with sunflower oil and line with parchment paper.

To make the puffs, bring the water, salt, and butter to a boil in a pan over a medium heat. Remove from the heat, add the flour and stir with a wooden spoon until well mixed. Return to the heat and beat for 1–2 minutes, until the mixture is smooth and pulls away from the sides. Off the heat, beat in the eggs, one at a time, making sure each egg is mixed in before adding the next. Beat until the mixture is smooth and glossy (it will be slightly sticky).

Drop tablespoonfuls of the mixture onto the baking sheet and put in a preheated oven, 350°F, for 25–30 minutes until puffed up.

Meanwhile, combine all the filling ingredients in a bowl.

To serve, remove the puffs from the oven and allow to cool. Split each one in half, spread a little cheese mixture on one half and top with the remaining half. Serve immediately.

Makes about 15

Puffs
sunflower oil, for greasing
$^3/_4$ cup water
pinch of salt
$^1/_3$ cup butter
1 cup all-purpose flour, sifted
3 eggs

Filling
4 oz Welsh goats' cheese (soft)
2 tablespoons cream cheese
3 tablespoons very finely chopped roasted red bell pepper (use canned or bottled)
1 tablespoon finely chopped chives
salt and pepper to taste

Goats' cheeses can range from very soft and spreadable to hard and crumbly. Welsh goats' cheese is renowned for its flavor and quality.

Crispy whitebait and French-fry cones   **25**

Line a large sheet of newspaper with waxed paper, cut the double layer into 12 squares and twist each into a small cone.

Rinse the fries in cold water and dry thoroughly on paper towels. Pour the oil into a deep-fat fryer to a depth of at least 3 inches and heat to 350°F. Deep-fry the fries for 4–5 minutes, then drain on paper towels and deep fry them again for 1–2 minutes until crisp and golden. Drain the fries and keep them warm in a preheated oven, 250°F.

To prepare the whitebait, heat the oil to 350°F. Put the flour on a large plate and season well with salt and pepper. Toss the fish in the flour and fry in batches for 1–2 minutes, or until crisp and golden. Drain on paper towels.

To serve, toss the whitebait with the French fries, season with sea salt and pile into the paper cones. Serve the malt vinegar on the side.

Makes 12 cones

French fries

8 oz potatoes, peeled and cut into
   long, thin fries
sunflower oil, for deep-frying
sea salt, for sprinkling
malt vinegar, to serve

Crispy whitebait

sunflower oil, for deep-frying
4 tablespoons all-purpose flour
12 oz whitebait (smelt)
salt and pepper

The **great** British **culinary** tradition of "**fish and chips**" actually **originated** as two **separate entities**, with the **French inventing** the fries.

26 Beefsteak tartare on endive scoops

Using a very sharp knife, very finely chop the beef and then grind it (or get your butcher to do this for you).

Put the meat into a food processor with the capers, onions, parsley, and anchovies and season well with pepper. Process until smooth.

Put the endive leaves onto a serving platter and spoon some of the tartare mixture onto the base of each leaf. Garnish with the parsley and serve the scoops immediately.

Variation
You could also serve the tartare mixture spooned onto dark rye bread, if desired.

Makes 20

8 oz very good-quality, lean beef tenderloin
2 tablespoons capers, very finely chopped
2 tablespoons very finely chopped onion
2 tablespoons very finely chopped parsley
4 canned anchovy fillets, drained and finely chopped
pepper
20 green or red endive leaves
parsley, to garnish

Beef or **steak tartare** is meat that is **ground**, highly seasoned and **eaten raw**. The **crunchy endive** leaves provide a **good contrast** in texture.

Rosemary and veal frikadeller skewers 29

Cook the potato in a saucepan of lightly salted, boiling water for about 15 minutes until tender. Drain and put in a large bowl, then allow to cool.

Mash the potato, then stir in the rosemary, sour cream, anchovy paste, allspice, olive oil, bread crumbs, red onion, garlic, and veal. Season well with salt and pepper and mash to combine thoroughly. Divide the mixture into 25 portions and shape each one into a ball with your fingers. Arrange the balls on a nonstick baking sheet, cover with plastic wrap, and chill in the refrigerator for 2–3 hours.

When ready to cook the frikadellers, heat the oil in a large, nonstick skillet to 325°F and pan-fry the balls, in batches, for 5–6 minutes, or until browned. Drain each batch on paper towels.

Remove some of the leaves from each rosemary sprig, leaving about 1½ inches of leaves untouched at one end. To serve, skewer the frikadeller with the rosemary stems and accompany with lemon wedges and a bowl of mayonnaise.

Makes 25

1 medium potato, peeled and roughly chopped

1 teaspoon very finely chopped rosemary leaves

1 tablespoon sour cream

1 teaspoon anchovy paste

¼ teaspoon ground allspice

1 tablespoon olive oil

3 tablespoons natural dried bread crumbs

2 tablespoons very finely chopped red onion

1 garlic clove, crushed

12 oz finely ground veal

oil, for pan-frying

salt and pepper

To serve
25 rosemary sprigs, 3–4 inches long
lemon wedges
mayonnaise

Frikadeller are meatballs and made here with veal, a naturally lean meat popular in Holland. Before it was used as a flavoring for meat, rosemary was primarily a medicinal remedy for infections.

30 Broiled mussels with herbed beer butter

Put the mussels into a large saucepan with the beer. Cover the pan, place over a high heat and cook for 4–5 minutes, shaking the pan from time to time to ensure the mussels cook evenly. When all the mussels have opened, remove the pan from the heat and discard the top shell from each mussel. Discard any mussels that have not opened. Put the mussels on a rack in a single layer and set aside.

Mix the butter with the parsley, lemon zest, juice, and beer. Season well with salt and pepper and, using a small teaspoon, spoon some of the mixture on top of each mussel. Broil the mussels for 1–2 minutes, or until the butter has melted. Meanwhile, line a serving platter with sea salt— this will keep the mussels stable. Put the cooked mussels on the salt and serve immediately.

Makes 20

20 large, fresh mussels, scrubbed
$1/2$ cup Belgian beer
sea salt, for lining platter

Herbed beer butter
$1/2$ cup butter, softened
4 tablespoons finely chopped parsley
1 teaspoon thinly grated lemon zest
2 tablespoons lemon juice
2 tablespoons Belgian beer
salt and pepper

The **distinctly** Belgian partnership of a bowl of mussels and a tankard of beer is well known. Here they're combined to make a **decadent snack**.

FRANCE

Seared foie gras on French bread

Toast the bread on both sides until crisp and lightly browned. Lightly rub one side of each slice of toast with the garlic and put on a serving platter, rubbed-side up.

Heat the oil in a large, nonstick skillet until very hot. Add the foie gras and sear over a high heat for 2–3 minutes on each side. Remove the foie gras from the pan and, using a sharp knife, cut it into 12 slices. Put a slice on each piece of toast, season well with salt and pepper, and sprinkle some chopped tarragon over each one to garnish. Serve immediately.

Makes 12

12 thin slices of bread cut from a
  small French baguette 2–2½ inches
  in diameter
3–4 garlic cloves, halved
1 tablespoon olive oil
3–4 slices of foie gras, 10–12 oz in total
salt and pepper
very finely chopped tarragon, to garnish

Despite being a French delicacy, foie gras is believed to have originated in Egypt. Today it is an expensive luxury food served on special occasions.

34 Reblochon, tomato, and ham quichettes

Roll out the pastry on a lightly floured surface to an ⅛ inch thickness and use to line 20 mini tartlet pans 2–2½ inches in diameter. Prick the base of each quichette with a fork and chill for 30 minutes.

Line each tartlet shell with parchment paper and fill with pie weights. Put on a baking sheet in a preheated oven, 400°F, for 11–12 minutes until firm, then remove the paper and weights and return to the oven for 8–10 minutes, or until crisp and golden. Remove from the oven and let cool on a wire rack.

Meanwhile, put the Reblochon in a freezer and chill until firm, then cut into as small dice as possible.

Divide the ham between the cooled quichette shells and top each one with cherry tomato quarters and the cheese. Return to the oven for 6–8 minutes, or until the cheese has melted and the tarts are golden. Remove from the oven and garnish with rosemary sprigs before serving.

Makes 20

10 oz shortcrust pastry, thawed if frozen

Filling
5 oz Reblochon cheese
3 tablespoons very finely chopped ham
8 cherry tomatoes, quartered
small rosemary sprigs, to garnish

Reblochon is a mild mountain cheese. The name refers to the creamy cow's milk that is specially selected for the production of the cheese.

Raclette fondue with baby potato dippers **37**

Cook the potatoes in a large saucepan of lightly salted, boiling water for 10–12 minutes, or until just tender. Drain and set aside.

Rub the garlic around the interior of a medium-size fondue pot. Discard the garlic. Put the Raclette and milk in the pot and heat gently over a low heat, stirring continuously with a wooden spoon. When the cheese starts to melt and the mixture becomes smooth and creamy, gradually add the wine and Kirsch. Season well with salt and pepper and heat the fondue through without boiling.

Use fondue forks or skewers to dip the boiled potatoes into the cheese mixture, and then eat them immediately.

Serves 4–6

1½ lb baby new potatoes, scrubbed
2 garlic cloves, sliced in half
1 lb Raclette cheese, diced
1 cup milk
¾ cup dry white wine
1 tablespoon Kirsch
salt and white pepper

Harsh winters traditionally isolated many Swiss country people and when the summer bread and cheese became dry and hard, the fondue was created to make them more enjoyable.

38 Mini schinkenfleckerin

Break the noodles into small pieces about 1½ inches long and cook according to the package instructions. Drain and set aside.

Line an 8-inch square, nonstick cake pan with parchment paper.

Heat the butter and oil in a large skillet and, when hot, add the onions. Cook, stirring, over a medium heat for 6–8 minutes until softened.

Beat the eggs with the sour cream in a bowl. Stir in the ham, cooked noodles, and onions, season well with salt and pepper and spoon the mixture into the prepared cake pan. Cover with foil and put in a preheated oven, 375°F, for 45 minutes. Remove the foil and bake for another 10–15 minutes, or until the mixture is set and firm. Remove from the oven and allow to cool completely. To serve, cut into bite-size squares.

Serves 4–6

8 oz dried thin egg noodles
1 tablespoon butter
1 tablespoon olive oil
1 small onion, finely chopped
4 eggs, lightly beaten
6 tablespoons sour cream
8 oz cooked ham, finely diced
salt and pepper

This **unusual combination** of cured ham and **noodles** is usually **served** as a casserole in Austria. **Some versions** are **flavored** with **spices**.

Mini beef goulash and gherkin pies 41

Heat the oil in a nonstick pan over a medium heat and cook the onion, stirring, until softened. Increase the heat to high, add the beef and stir-fry until sealed and lightly browned.

Add the garlic, tomato paste, paprika, and caraway seeds and cook, stirring, for 1–2 minutes. Add the stock and bring to a boil, then cover tightly and simmer over a very low heat for 2 hours, stirring occasionally. When the stock has reduced and the meat is very tender, remove from the heat and allow to cool completely. Stir in the sour cream and gherkins, season with salt and set aside.

Roll out the pastry to a ¼ inch thickness. Cut out 12 rounds with a 3 inch round cutter and 12 rounds with a 2½ inch cutter. Line a 12-hole mini muffin pan with the large rounds, and fill with teaspoons of the goulash. Cover the filling, pressing the edges to seal. Brush with beaten egg. Put in a preheated oven, 400°F, for 30 minutes. Cool the pies on wire racks. Serve warm.

Makes 12

1 tablespoon olive oil
1 small onion, finely chopped
8 oz beef tenderloin, cut into
 ½ inch cubes
1 garlic clove, crushed
1 tablespoon tomato paste
1 tablespoon paprika
1 teaspoon caraway seeds
2 cups beef stock
1 tablespoon sour cream
1 tablespoon chopped gherkins
12 oz shortcrust pastry
beaten egg, for glazing
salt

Hungarian **herdsmen** traditionally prepared goulash as they drove their cattle to the **big markets** of Europe.

42 Blinis with sour cream and caviar

To make the blinis, sift the flours and salt into a large bowl and make a well in the center. Beat the egg yolk with the cream and milk and gradually pour into the well. Draw the flour into the egg mixture and mix to a smooth batter. Put the egg whites in a separate bowl and beat until softly peaked, then, using a metal spoon, fold into the flour mixture and mix until just combined.

Brush a large, nonstick skillet with a little oil and put over a medium heat. When hot, add heaped teaspoonfuls of the batter, in batches, and cook for about 3 minutes until bubbles appear on the surface. Flip the blinis over and cook for another 1–2 minutes, or until cooked through. Remove each batch from the skillet and put on waxed paper to cool. Brush the skillet with oil in between batches.

To serve, arrange the blinis on a serving platter and top with small spoonfuls of sour cream and caviar or roe. Just before serving, sprinkle the egg and the dill on the blinis, then season with pepper and serve.

Makes 20

Blinis

1/2 cup buckwheat flour

1/3 cup self-rising flour

pinch of salt

1 egg, separated

3 tablespoons light cream

1/2 cup milk

sunflower oil, for frying

Topping

about 1/2 cup thick, sour cream

5 oz Russian caviar or
    salmon roe

1 tablespoon very finely chopped
    hard-cooked egg

1 tablespoon very finely chopped dill

pepper

Authentic caviar is the roe of the sturgeon; most caviar today comes from the Caspian Sea. In Russia, blinis (pancakes) are often accompanied by chilled vodka.

Zucchini flower fritters

Carefully clean the zucchini flowers and discard the stamens.

Sift the flour, baking powder, and salt into a bowl. Gradually add the beer, beating continuously until you have a smooth, slightly thick batter.

Heat the oil in a large, deep, heavy skillet until it reaches 325°F. Working carefully and quickly, dip the zucchini flowers into the batter, a few at a time, and lower into the hot oil. Fry each batch for 5–6 minutes, turning once, until lightly golden and crisp. Remove with a slotted spoon and drain on paper towels.

Serve the zucchini flower fritters immediately, sprinkled with a little extra sea salt, if using.

Makes 15

15 zucchini flowers
1 cup very fine Italian all-purpose flour (tipo 0)
1 teaspoon baking powder
large pinch of salt
1 cup chilled beer
sunflower oil, for deep-frying
sea salt, for sprinkling (optional)

The life of a **zucchini flower** is short and they are **best** prepared no more than **two days** after being **harvested.**

46 Proscuitto and scallop spiedini

Put the garlic into a small bowl, mix in the chili, olive oil, orange juice, and oregano and season with salt.

Arrange the scallops in a single layer in a shallow bowl and pour over the garlic and chili mixture. Cover and let marinate for 15–20 minutes.

Cut each slice of proscuitto into 2 strips. Wrap a strip of proscuitto around each scallop and secure with a metal skewer or presoaked bamboo skewer. Add a basil leaf and a tomato half to each skewer.

Preheat the broiler to high. Position the skewers about 2½ inches away from the heat and cook for 1–2 minutes on each side or until the scallops have just cooked through—do not overcook or the scallops will become tough.

Remove from the oven and serve immediately.

Makes 20

2 garlic cloves, crushed

1 dried red chili, crushed

4 tablespoons olive oil

juice of ½ orange

1 teaspoon dried oregano

20 large scallops, with or without the coral (roe)

10 thin slices of proscuitto

salt

Garnish

20 basil leaves

20 sun-blushed tomato halves

Proscuitto is a **cured ham** that is **salted** for about two months before **being hung** until it has **dried completely**. Spiedini are Italian kabobs.

Manchego and membrillo bites   **49**

Cut the membrillo or quince cheese into 15 bite-size cubes or pieces and set aside.

Put the egg whites in a clean bowl and, using an electric or hand beater, beat until softly peaked. Fold in the Manchego, bread crumbs and parsley, then season with salt and pepper and form the mixture into 15 bite-size balls.

Heat the oil in a large, deep skillet to 350°F and fry the balls in batches for 2–3 minutes, or until golden brown and crisp. Drain on paper towels and keep each batch warm until all the balls have been cooked.

To serve, skewer a piece of the membrillo or quince cheese with a Manchego ball on a toothpick and serve immediately.

Makes 15

5 oz membrillo or firm quince cheese

2 egg whites

4 oz mature Manchego cheese, grated

1½ cups fresh white bread crumbs

2 tablespoons finely chopped flat leaf parsley

sunflower oil, for deep frying

salt and pepper

Manchego, made from **sheep's milk**, is the most **well-known** Spanish cheese. **Membrillo** is a **jelly or paste** made from **quinces**.

50 Green pea, potato, and mint tortilla bites

Cook the potato in a saucepan of lightly salted, boiling water for about 15 minutes, or until just tender. Drain and set aside.

Heat the oil in a medium, nonstick skillet over a medium heat and add the onion. Cook, stirring constantly, for 4–5 minutes, then add the garlic and drained potato. Cook, stirring, for 1–2 minutes, then add the peas and beaten eggs and season well with salt and pepper. Scatter in the mint. Turn the heat to low and cook for 10–12 minutes, or until the bottom of the tortilla is set and browned.

Put the tortilla under a medium-hot broiler and cook until the top is set and lightly browned. Remove from the heat and allow to cool for 20 minutes before turning out onto a clean surface. Cut the tortilla into bite-size squares, triangles, or any other shapes you want and serve at room temperature.

Makes about 20

1 large potato, about 8 oz, peeled and cut into $1/2$ inch squares
2 tablespoons Spanish olive oil
1 small onion, very finely chopped
1 garlic clove, finely chopped
$2^2/_3$ cups frozen peas, thawed
6 large eggs, lightly beaten
3 tablespoons chopped mint
salt and pepper

Regular tortillas are made only with eggs, while **tortilla Espanola**, or Spanish omelet, includes potatoes and is served in **thick slices** for breakfast or lunch.

Pecorino shortbread rounds with pesto **53**

Line a baking sheet with parchment paper. To make the shortbread rounds, sift the flour into a bowl and, using your fingers, mix in the paprika, butter, and Pecorino until well combined. Knead for 4–5 minutes to form a smooth dough.

Roll out the dough on a lightly floured board to a ½ inch thickness and, using a 1½ inch round cookie or pastry cutter, stamp out 20 rounds. Carefully put the rounds on the baking sheet and chill in the refrigerator for 1 hour.

Put the baking sheet in a preheated oven, 350°F, for 8–10 minutes, or until the rounds are lightly browned. Remove from the oven and allow to cool on a wire rack until crisp and firm.

Meanwhile, put all the ingredients for the pesto in a food processor or blender and pulse to a thick paste.

To serve, put the shortbread rounds on a serving platter, top each one with a spoonful of the pesto and garnish with some diced tomato and a basil leaf.

Makes 20

Shortbread rounds
½ **cup all-purpose flour, sifted**
pinch of paprika
2 tablespoons cold butter, diced
1½ **oz Pecorino cheese, finely grated**

Pesto
1 garlic clove, crushed
⅓ **cup basil**
2 tablespoons pine nuts
5 tablespoons finely grated Pecorino cheese
2 tablespoons olive oil

Garnish
finely diced tomato
small basil leaves

Sardinia has a history of **cheese-making** and **Pecorino**, a **hard cheese** similar to **Parmesan**, is one of the country's **specialties**. Pesto originated in the Ligurian port of **Genoa**.

Greek phyllo and nut baklavas

To make the syrup, put all the ingredients into a pan and bring to a boil. Reduce the heat and simmer gently for 15 minutes until thickened slightly. Remove from the heat and allow to cool, then chill in the refrigerator for 4–5 hours or overnight.

To make the baklava, grease an 8 x 12 inch nonstick jellyroll pan with the oil. Mix the nuts, cardamom, and sugar. Brush 4 sheets of the phyllo with some melted butter and place on top of each other. Fold in half lengthwise and use to line the prepared pan, trimming the pastry if necessary. Sprinkle one third of the nut mixture over the phyllo, then repeat twice with the remaining phyllo and nut mixture to give 3 layers of nut mixture and 4 of phyllo. Brush the top with the remaining butter and score into large, bite-size diamonds. Put in a preheated oven, 350°F, for 30–35 minutes or until golden and crisp. Pour over the chilled syrup, then cover and refrigerate overnight.

To serve, cut the baklava into diamonds.

Serves 10–12

Spiced sugar syrup

2 cups superfine sugar
¼ teaspoon ground cloves
1 teaspoon ground cinnamon
1 teaspoon thinly grated lemon zest
1 teaspoon thinly grated orange zest
2 cups water

Baklava

sunflower oil, for greasing
1²⁄₃ cups almonds, finely chopped
1²⁄₃ cups walnuts, finely chopped
1 teaspoon ground cardamom
½ cup superfine sugar
16 large sheets of phyllo pastry
¾ cup butter, melted

This **rich dish** with its **paper-thin pastry** was **being prepared** in the kitchens of Greece's **elite families** as long ago as 300BC.

AFRICA

58 Lemon and couscous-stuffed tomatoes

Cut the tomatoes in half and, using a small spoon, scoop out and discard the seeds. Put the tomato shells, cut-side down, on a piece of paper towel and set aside.

Put the couscous in a small heatproof bowl, stir in the oil and pour over boiling water to just cover. Cover with plastic wrap and let rest for 8—10 minutes to absorb the water.

Meanwhile, finely dice the preserved lemon, discarding any seeds. Fluff up the couscous with a fork, stir in the lemon and mint and season well with salt and pepper.

Put the tomato halves on a serving platter. Using a small teaspoon, spoon some of the couscous mixture into each tomato shell, garnish with mint leaves, if using, and serve at room temperature.

Makes 20

10 midi tomatoes, each about
 1½ inches in diameter
¼ cup couscous
2 tablespoons olive oil
1 preserved lemon
3 tablespoons finely chopped mint
salt and pepper
tiny mint leaves, to garnish (optional)

Preserved lemons are used in all kinds of Moroccan dishes—they provide an almost creamy citrus flavor and go well with chicken, lamb, and vegetables.

Crisp almond and sesame samsa   **61**

Bring three quarters of the sugar and all the water to a boil in a small pan. Reduce the heat to low and stir until the sugar has dissolved. Add the lemon juice, bring to a boil and boil rapidly for 10 minutes until syrupy. Remove from the heat and allow to cool. Stir in half the orange flower water.

Line a baking sheet with parchment paper. Knead the ground almonds to a paste with the orange zest, cinnamon, the remaining sugar, and orange flower water. Cut the phyllo into 24 long strips 2½ inches wide. Brush a strip with melted butter, put a small spoonful of almond filling at the bottom, fold over the sides and roll up the pastry along its length. Repeat with the remaining strips. Put the parcels on the baking sheet and brush with melted butter. Put in a preheated oven, 350°F, for 15–18 minutes, until golden.

Remove the pastries from the oven and place in a single layer in a dish. Pour over the syrup and leave for 3–4 minutes. Lift the pastries onto a serving platter; sprinkle over the sesame seeds. Let cool.

Makes 24

²/₃ cup superfine sugar
1¼ cups water
2 tablespoons lemon juice
2 tablespoons orange flower water
2 cups ground almonds
thinly grated zest of 1 small orange
1½ teaspoons ground cinnamon
about 5 oz phyllo pastry
melted butter, for brushing
4 tablespoons lightly toasted sesame
    seeds

Like most North African pastries, these crisp samsa from Tunisia are very sweet. Orange flower water is frequently used to flavor pastries and desserts.

62 Smoky eggplant dip with crudités

Using a pair of tongs to protect your hand, hold each eggplant over an open flame until lightly charred all over—each one will take about 10 minutes. Carefully put the eggplants on a nonstick baking sheet and put in a preheated oven, 400°F, for 30–40 minutes, or until soft and slightly collapsed. Remove from the oven.

When cool enough to handle, hold each eggplant by the stalk over a bowl and carefully strip off and discard the skin, saving any juice in the bowl. Put the pulp, while still warm, and any juice in a food processor or blender and pulse to mash roughly. Add the garlic, lemon juice, and tahini and process to a smooth paste. Season with salt and cayenne and allow to cool, then cover and chill for a few hours before serving.

To serve, put the puree in a shallow dipping bowl and drizzle over some olive oil and cayenne pepper. Serve with the vegetable crudités to dip into it.

Serves 4–6

2 large eggplants
2 garlic cloves, crushed
juice of 2 lemons
1 tablespoon tahini
salt and freshly ground cayenne pepper
olive oil, for drizzling

To serve
red radishes, trimmed
scallions, trimmed
celery, carrot, and cucumber strips

This recipe takes the Egyptian dip baba ghanoush as its inspiration. In Egypt breads and dips are eaten as snacks or as part of the main meal.

Peanut ice cream in phyllo shells   **65**

Put all the ingredients for the ice cream into an ice-cream machine and follow the manufacturer's instructions, then place the ice cream in a shallow, freezer container and freeze until ready to use.

Alternatively, put all the ice-cream ingredients into a large bowl and, using an electric or hand beater, beat for 3–4 minutes. Pour this mixture into a shallow freezer container, cover and freeze for 3–4 hours, or until semi-frozen. Remove from the freezer, transfer to a blender and pulse for a few seconds until the mixture is smooth but slushy. Return it to the container and freeze for 2–3 hours, or until almost firm. Repeat the process of blending and freezing twice more, so three times in all.

Meanwhile, make the phyllo shells (see page 131) and let cool completely.

To serve, put the phyllo shells on a platter. Remove the ice cream from the freezer and let soften slightly, then fill each shell. Garnish with chopped peanuts, dust with confectioners' sugar and serve at once.

Makes 20

Ice cream
2½ cups ready-made fresh custard
1½ cups roasted peanuts, finely
    chopped, plus extra to garnish
few drops of vanilla extract

Phyllo shells
7 oz phyllo pastry, thawed if frozen
¼ cup butter, melted
confectioners' sugar, for dusting

Almost half of all the cultivated land in Senegal is devoted to the production of peanuts, which are also known as groundnuts.

66 Sweet potato pone

Boil the sweet potatoes unpeeled for 10–15 minutes until tender, then peel and cut into small cubes.

Line the base and sides of a 9 inch square cake pan with parchment paper. While the potatoes are still warm, stir in the sugar, butter, and cream, then add the ginger, cinnamon, cloves, and orange flower water and stir to mix. Beat the egg yolks and stir in. Using an electric or hand beater, beat the egg whites to soft peaks and fold in.

Spoon the mixture into the prepared pan, smooth the top and put in a preheated oven, 400°F, for 20 minutes. Reduce the heat to 300°F, and bake for a further 20–25 minutes, or until set and firm to touch. Remove from the oven and allow to cool completely, before turning out of the pan.

To serve, cut the pone into bite-size diamond shapes or squares and dust with confectioners' sugar, if using.

Serves 4–6

1 lb sweet potatoes
$^1/_3$ cup dark brown sugar
2 tablespoons butter
3 tablespoons heavy cream
2 teaspoons ground ginger
1 teaspoon ground cinnamon
pinch of ground cloves
1 tablespoon orange flower water
3 large egg yolks
2 egg whites
confectioners' sugar, for dusting
   (optional)

Sweet potato and ginger are used extensively in Liberian cuisine. Pone can be served either hot or cold and is eaten as a snack.

Maschi canapés

Cut the cucumbers in half lengthwise and, using a small spoon, scoop out and discard the seeds. Cut the cucumber into 20 x 2 inch long pieces or "boats." Lightly sprinkle with salt and put them cut-side down on paper towels.

Cut the roast beef into small dice and put in a bowl with the rice, dill, tomato, and olive oil. Season with salt and pepper and stir to mix well.

To assemble the canapés, put the cucumber "boats" on a serving platter and stuff each one with a heaped teaspoonful of the beef and rice mixture. Serve at room temperature.

Makes 20

2 large, long cucumbers

2 oz sliced roast beef

10 tablespoons cooked white rice

6 tablespoons finely chopped dill

1 tablespoon finely diced tomato

1 tablespoon olive oil

salt and pepper

This recipe is an adaptation of Maschi, which is a traditional Sudanese dish of tomatoes stuffed with beef and flavored with spices.

70 Lab with toasted flat-bread dippers

Put the cream and feta cheeses into a bowl and mix until fairly smooth.

Heat the butter in a small, nonstick skillet and when hot and foaming add the onion and garlic. Cook, stirring, for 3–4 minutes over a high heat, then stir in the turmeric, cardamom seeds, and cinnamon and cook for 1 minute. Remove from the heat and add the lemon zest. Stir to mix well, then pour this into the cheese mixture and stir to combine. Season well with salt and pepper, garnish with parsley, and serve immediately with grilled or toasted flat-bread strips.

Serves 6–8

$1^2/_3$ cups lowfat cream cheese

4 oz feta cheese, crumbled

1 tablespoon butter

2 tablespoons very finely chopped onion

2 garlic cloves, finely chopped

$1/_4$ teaspoon ground turmeric

1 teaspoon cardamom seeds

$1/_2$ teaspoon ground cinnamon

2 teaspoons thinly grated lemon zest

salt and pepper

chopped parsley, to garnish

2–3 flat breads, cut into thin strips and grilled or toasted until crisp, to serve

Lab is an Ethiopian curd cheese, seasoned with a range of herbs and spices. Here we have replicated its particular acid flavor by mixing feta cheese with lowfat cream cheese.

Oyster Mombasa

Combine all the ingredients for the topping in a small bowl and let stand at room temperature for 30 minutes.

Meanwhile, shuck the oysters. Wash the 20 bottom shells and dry with paper towels. Line a serving platter with a bed of **sea** salt, put the oyster shells on it and set aside.

Carefully dip the oysters into the seasoned flour, then into the beaten egg, and then into the dried bread crumbs, to coat evenly.

Heat the oil in a large, deep saucepan to 375°F and, working in batches, deep-fry the oysters for 1–2 minutes, or until lightly golden and crisp on the outside (the oysters should remain soft inside). Drain each batch on paper towels while you fry the remainder.

To serve, put each fried oyster on each prepared oyster shell and spoon over a little of the garlic and chili topping. Serve immediately.

Makes 20

20 large fresh oysters
sea salt, for lining platter
6 tablespoons seasoned flour
2 eggs, lightly beaten
1³/₄ cups natural dried bread crumbs
sunflower oil, for deep-frying

Topping
2 garlic cloves, very finely diced
2 red chilies, seeded and very finely
   sliced or diced
3 tablespoons very finely chopped parsley
juice of 3 limes
2 tablespoons light olive oil
salt

Kenya is renowned for its **oysters** and this is a **typical way** to **prepare** and **serve** them, either as a **snack** or a **starter**.

74 Cocktail spice island fish cakes

Cook the potatoes in lightly salted, boiling water for about 15 minutes, or until just tender, then drain thoroughly. Put the fish in a food processor or blender and roughly pulse. Add the potatoes to the fish with the spices, lemon zest and juice, season with salt and pepper and process briefly until just combined. Transfer to a bowl and mix to a firm consistency. Divide the mixture into 20 portions and form into balls.

Spread the bread crumbs on a large plate and roll each ball in them, to cover completely. Put the balls on a nonstick tray and press down lightly on each one to form a cake. Cover and chill overnight.

When ready to cook, lightly grease a baking sheet and line with parchment paper. Transfer the fish cakes to the baking sheet and drizzle over a little oil. Put in a preheated oven, 400°F, for 10–12 minutes until lightly golden and cooked through, then remove from the oven and allow to cool to room temperature before serving.

Makes 20

8 oz potatoes, peeled and roughly chopped
8 oz halibut or cod fillet, roughly chopped
1 teaspoon crushed saffron threads
$1/4$ teaspoon ground cloves
2 teaspoons ground cumin
2 teaspoons ground cayenne pepper
$1/2$ teaspoon ground coriander
1 teaspoon fennel seeds
thinly grated zest and juice of 1 lemon
natural dried bread crumbs, for coating
olive oil, for drizzling
salt and pepper

Cloves were the first spice to be introduced to Zanzibar. They thrived and more spices followed, leading to the country's nickname of "The Spice Island."

Piri-piri chicken drumettes 77

To prepare the chicken wings to make the drumettes, cut through the first joint of each wing and discard the wing tips. Holding the small end of the second joint, cut and gently scrape the chicken meat down toward the thick end of the wing. Pull the skin and meat over the end of the bone with your fingers, to resemble a baby chicken drumstick, then, using a sharp knife or kitchen scissors, trim off the knuckle end of the exposed bone. Repeat with the remaining wings. Arrange the wings in a single layer in a shallow, nonreactive dish.

Mix all the ingredients for the marinade and pour over the drumettes. Toss to coat evenly, cover and marinate overnight in the refrigerator.

When ready to cook, line a baking sheet with parchment paper. Put the chicken drumettes on the baking sheet and put in a preheated oven, 350°F, for 25–30 minutes, or until cooked through. Remove from the oven and serve immediately with wedges of lemon to squeeze over.

Makes 20

20 large chicken wings
lemon wedges, to serve

Piri-piri marinade
4 tablespoons olive oil
2 garlic cloves, crushed
2 teaspoons grated fresh ginger root
4 tablespoons piri-piri sauce or
    hot chili sauce
1 tablespoon honey
juice of 3 lemons
salt to taste

The **piri-piri** chili pepper is believed to have been **introduced** to Mozambique by the Portuguese. The word is Swahili and means "**pepper-pepper.**"

78 Mini bobotie open pies

Put the pastry on a lightly floured surface and stamp out 24 circles with a 3 in round pastry cutter. Line 24 nonstick mini muffin pan holes with the pastry, pressing it down to fit neatly. Cover and chill in the refrigerator until ready to cook.

Heat the oil in a pan, add the onion, beef, and spices and stir-fry over a high heat for 3–4 minutes. Add the tomato paste and beef stock. Bring to a boil, then reduce the heat to low, cover the pan and cook for 10–15 minutes, stirring occasionally, until the meat is just tender and the liquid has evaporated. Season with salt and pepper and set aside to cool.

Spoon teaspoonfuls of the cooled beef mixture into the pastry cases to come halfway up the sides.

Beat the eggs, nutmeg, and cream, season with salt and pepper and carefully pour this mixture over the mince to just cover. Place in a preheated oven, 400°F, for 12–15 minutes, or until the tops are set. Leave the pies to cool for 10 minutes then turn out of the pans and serve.

Makes 24

3 sheets ready-rolled shortcrust pastry, thawed if frozen

flour, for dusting

1 tablespoon olive oil

1 tablespoon finely chopped red onion

8 oz ground beef

$\frac{1}{4}$ teaspoon allspice

$\frac{1}{2}$ teaspoon ground cinnamon

$\frac{1}{2}$ teaspoon ground coriander

1 tablespoon tomato paste

3 tablesoons beef stock

2 large eggs

pinch of nutmeg

3 tablespoons light cream

salt and pepper

South African cuisine has evolved to incorporate elements from the many nationalities who have lived in the country over the years. Bobotie is a popular Cape Malay dish.

ASIA

82 Spicy pea and potato samosas

First make the filling. Heat the ghee or oil in a large, nonstick skillet. Add the garlic and red chili and stir-fry for 1 minute, then add the spices and stir-fry for 20–30 seconds. Add the potatoes and peas and stir-fry over a medium heat for 4–5 minutes. Remove from the heat and stir in the fresh cilantro. Season with salt and set aside to cool.

Line a baking sheet with parchment paper. Roll out the pastry to a ¼ inch thickness. Using a 5 inch round pastry cutter, stamp out 10 disks. Cut each one in half and form into a semi-circular cone. Overlap and roughen the two edges and wet them to seal. Fill each cone with a little filling, then wet the top and crimp the edges to seal completely. Repeat to make 20 mini samosas.

Place the samosas on the baking sheet, brush lightly with melted ghee or butter and put in a preheated oven, 400°F, for 20–25 minutes. Remove from the oven and serve warm, with ketchup for dipping, if desired.

Makes 20

12 oz shortcrust pastry, thawed if frozen
a little melted ghee or butter, for brushing

Filling

2 tablespoons ghee or sunflower oil, plus
   extra for brushing
3 garlic cloves, finely chopped
1 red chili, seeded and finely chopped
2 teaspoons cumin seeds
2 teaspoons ground cumin
1 teaspoon ground cilantro
¼ teaspoon turmeric
10 oz potatoes, boiled until tender and
   cut into ½ inch dice
1⅓ cups fresh or frozen peas
6 tablespoons finely chopped fresh
   cilantro
salt
spicy tomato ketchup, to serve (optional)

Samosas are traditional Indian snacks that combine vegetables and spices in a dough pocket that's fried until crispy.

Onion and gram flour fritters 85

Place all the ingredients for the dip in a blender and process until fairly smooth. Transfer to a bowl and chill until ready to serve.

Sift both flours into a large bowl and add the spices. Season with salt, then pour in enough cold water—about ¾ cup—to make a thick, pourable batter. Add the onion slices and mix well until you have a thick mixture.

Pour the oil into a large, deep saucepan to one-third full and heat to 350°F. Working in batches, carefully lower large teaspoonfuls of the onion mixture into the oil and fry for 3–4 minutes, or until crisp and golden. Remove each batch with a slotted spoon and drain on paper towels while you fry the next batch, keeping the fritters warm.

To serve, place the fritters on a platter with the bowl of dip in the center.

Serves 4–6

2 cups gram flour or besan flour
1 tablespoon rice flour
2 tablespoons crushed cilantro seeds
1 teaspoon chili powder
¼ teaspoon turmeric
2–3 onions, halved and very thinly sliced
sunflower oil, for deep-frying
salt

Coconut and mint chutney dip
1 cup freshly grated coconut meat
1 green chili, seeded and chopped
small handful of chopped mint
¾ cup thick plain yogurt
1 teaspoon sugar
1 teaspoon salt

Also known as **chickpea** flour, **gram** flour is used **extensively** in Indian cooking. It is **high in protein**, which benefits the largely **vegetarian population**.

86 Steamed Chinese purses

Place all the ingredients for the filling in a food processor or blender and process until well combined. Transfer to a bowl, cover and chill for 4–5 hours or overnight.

Using a 2½ inch round cookie or pastry cutter, stamp out rounds from each wonton wrapper. Place a heaped teaspoonful of the filling in the center of a wonton round and press down gently to spread the filling almost to the edges. Place the filled round in the palm of your hand and then cup your hand, pressing the filling down with your thumb to make an open cup or purse. Tap the base gently on a clean surface to make a flat base and neaten the top with your fingers. Repeat to make 20 purses.

Line 3 layers of a bamboo steamer with parchment paper and arrange the purses on them. Cover and steam over a wok or saucepan of boiling water for 8–10 minutes, or until cooked through. Serve the purses immediately with soy dipping sauce.

Makes 20

20 fresh wonton wrappers, each
    3 inches square
soy dipping sauce, to serve

Filling
4 oz ground chicken
4 oz raw shrimp, chopped
1 teaspoon crushed Szechuan pepper
1 egg white
1 teaspoon sesame oil
1 teaspoon finely grated garlic
1 teaspoon finely grated fresh
    ginger root
1 teaspoon dark soy sauce
2 tablespoons finely chopped chives

Steaming is a popular method of cooking in China, and these little "purses" or buns are well liked.

Salt and chili squid

Open out the squid tubes and pat dry with paper towels. Lay them on a cutting board, shiny-side down, and, using a sharp knife, lightly score a fine diamond pattern on the flesh, being careful not to cut all the way through. Cut the squid into 2 x 1 inch pieces and place in a nonreactive dish. Pour over the lemon juice, cover and chill for 15 minutes.

Fill a wok one-third full with oil and heat to 350°F. Combine the cornstarch, salt, pepper, chili powder, and sugar in a bowl. Dip the squid pieces into the beaten egg white and then into the cornstarch mixture, shaking off any excess.

Deep-fry the squid, in batches, for 1 minute, or until it turns pale golden and curls up. Remove each batch with a slotted spoon and drain on paper towels.

Mix all the ingredients for the dipping sauce in a bowl. Serve the squid in small paper cones, if desired, garnished with sliced red chili and scallions and accompanied by the dipping sauce.

Serves 6–8

1½ lb squid tubes, halved lengthwise
¾ cup lemon juice
⅔ cup cornstarch
1½ tablespoons salt
2 teaspoons white pepper
1 teaspoon chili powder
2 teaspoons superfine sugar
4 egg whites, lightly beaten
sunflower oil, for deep-frying

Garnish
finely sliced red chilies
finely sliced scallions

Dipping sauce
1 red chili, seeded and finely diced
1 tablespoon very finely diced shallot
2 teaspoons very finely chopped fresh cilantro
6 tablespoons light soy sauce
1 tablespoon Chinese rice wine

Seafood is eaten with **great regularity** in China and **squid** will **often be served** as a **snack** or a **side dish** as part of a meal.

THAILAND

Chili beef and lime lettuce wraps

Heat the oil in a nonstick skillet or wok and when hot add the beef, garlic, lemon grass, lime leaves, scallions, and chilies. Stir-fry over a high heat for 5–6 minutes, or until the beef is sealed and lightly browned.

Add the soy sauce and stock and bring back to a boil. Cook over a moderate heat for 8–10 minutes, stirring often, until all the liquid has been absorbed. Remove from the heat and allow to cool. When cool, stir in the cucumber.

Mix the lime juice with the fish sauce and sugar and stir until the sugar has dissolved. Spoon this mixture over the beef and toss to mix well.

To serve, arrange the lettuce leaves on a serving platter and spoon 1 tablespoonful of the beef mixture into each of them. Garnish with the chili and lime leaf slivers and scatter over some chopped peanuts. Serve immediately.

Makes 20

1 tablespoon sunflower oil
8 oz ground beef
2 garlic cloves, finely chopped
1 tablespoon finely chopped lemon grass
4 kaffir lime leaves, finely shredded
2 scallions, finely sliced
2 red chilies, seeded and finely chopped
1 tablespoon dark soy sauce
$\frac{1}{2}$ cup chicken stock
4 tablespoons finely diced cucumber
juice of 2 limes
1 tablespoon Thai fish sauce
1 teaspoon superfine sugar
20 small crisp lettuce leaves

Garnish
slivers of red chili
kaffir lime leaves, finely shredded
chopped roasted peanuts

Kaffir lime leaves add an intense citrus zing to sweet and spicy dishes.

Fragrant shrimp and herb rolls

Cut the shrimp in half lengthwise, devein, clean and set aside. Combine the mint, cilantro, and scallion in a small bowl.

Soak the rice paper rounds, one at a time, in a bowl of cold water and leave to soften for 2–3 minutes. Carefully remove, then drain on a clean dish towel and cut each in half.

To assemble the rolls, place a half sheet of rice paper on a clean surface and top with a heaped teaspoonful of the herb mixture and one halved shrimp. Fold the rice paper over to enclose the filling, then place another halved shrimp, cut-side down, on top and continue to roll into a tight cylinder. Press the ends with a wet finger to seal. Place the roll, seam-side down, on a serving platter and cover with a dampened dish towel to keep moist while you make the rest.

Once prepared, serve immediately with sweet chili sauce and light soy sauce to dip into.

Makes 20

20 jumbo shrimp
1/4 cup mint, roughly chopped
1/4 cup fresh cilantro, roughly chopped
1 scallion, very finely chopped
10 rounds of rice paper, about 6 inches
   in diameter
sweet chili sauce and soy sauce,
   for dipping

Rice paper is made not from rice but from the pith of a small Chinese tree. When soaked it becomes strong and pliable.

94 Chili crab on mini noodle nests

Lightly grease 20 nonstick mini tartlet cases with sunflower oil. Divide the noodles into 20 portions and press each portion into a tartlet case to form a tartlet shape, making sure the base is covered. Lightly brush with more oil and put in a preheated oven, 350°F, for 8–10 minutes, or until crisp and firm. Remove from the cases and allow to cool on a wire rack.

To make the chili crab, heat the oil in a large nonstick wok or skillet and when hot add the scallions, garlic, ginger, and chili and stir-fry for 2–3 minutes. Add the crab and stir-fry for another 1–2 minutes, then remove from the heat, stir in the chili sauce and cilantro and toss to mix well.

To serve, place a heaped teaspoonful of the chili crab mixture into each cooled noodle nest and serve immediately.

Makes 20

Noodle nests
4 oz fresh, fine egg noodles
sunflower oil, for greasing

Chili crab
1 tablespoon sunflower oil
2 scallions, finely sliced
2 garlic cloves, finely chopped
1 teaspoon finely diced fresh ginger root
1 red chili, seeded and finely diced
7 oz fresh white crab meat
2 tablespoons sweet chili sauce
4 tablespoons finely chopped fresh
   cilantro

A **Singaporean favorite** that was **first eaten** in the 1950s when it was **sold** from a small stall. Its **popularity** spread and the dish is **served** in many of the **city's cafés** and restaurants **today**.

Gado gado

Bring a large saucepan of lightly salted water to a boil, add the carrots and green beans and blanch for 2–3 minutes. Drain and refresh in cold water. Cook the potatoes in lightly salted, boiling water for about 15 minutes, or until just tender, then drain and set aside. Arrange all the vegetables on a serving platter with the bean curd.

To make the spicy dipping sauce, combine all the ingredients in a small bowl.

To make the peanut sauce, mix the peanut butter with the chili and soy sauces and then pour in the boiling water and stir to mix well. Transfer to a dipping bowl.

Serve the vegetables with the two dipping sauces.

Serves 6–8

2 carrots, peeled and cut into thick, 2 inch long fingers

¾ cup long or green beans, cut into 2 inch lengths

2 large potatoes, peeled and cut into thick, 2 inch long fingers

1 cucumber, cut into thick, 2 inch long fingers

7 oz ready-prepared fried bean curd, cut into bite-size cubes

Spicy dipping sauce

2 tablespoons ketjap manis (sweet soy sauce)

1 tablespoons dark soy sauce

1 teaspoon sambal oelek (hot chili paste)

Peanut dipping sauce

4 tablespoons smooth peanut butter

2 tablespoons sweet chili sauce

3 tablespoons light soy sauce

3 tablespoons boiling water

This typical Indonesian dish is often served garnished with boiled egg and potatoes, making it a more filling main meal.

98 Soba, tobiko, and scallion spoons

Cook the dried soba noodles according to the package instructions until just tender. Drain and rinse in cold water.

Beat the soy sauce with the mirin, sesame oil, wasabi, and sunflower oil in a bowl until well blended. Add the noodles and toss gently to coat evenly, then stir in the scallions and toss to mix well.

To serve, divide the noodles into 20 bite-size portions and twirl each portion with a fork to make a neat nest. Carefully transfer to individual Oriental soup spoons, then, using a teaspoon, garnish each serving with a little tobiko or small salmon roe and serve immediately.

Makes 20

8 oz dried soba noodles
4 tablespoons light soy sauce
4 tablespoons mirin (rice wine)
1 teaspoon toasted sesame oil
1/4 teaspoon wasabi paste
6 tablespoons sunflower oil
2 scallions, very finely sliced
1 oz tobiko (flying fish roe)
   or small salmon roe

Tobiko is the small, red-orange, crunchy roe of the flying fish, often served with sushi dishes. Here it's a topping for soba noodles, which are made from buckwheat flour.

AUSTRALASIA

102 Damper squares with lemon myrtle

Line a large baking sheet with parchment paper and dust lightly with flour.

Put the flour, lemon myrtle, sugar, and salt into a large bowl and pour in the butter. Gradually add the milk and mix to make a medium soft dough.

Pat the dough into a 9 inch square and put it on the baking sheet. Brush with the egg glaze and put in a preheated oven, 400°F, for 30–35 minutes, or until golden and cooked through. Remove the damper from the oven and allow to cool on a wire rack.

Cut the damper into bite-size squares and serve accompanied by whipped cream and jam.

Serves 4–6

4 cups self-rising flour, sifted

2 teaspoons ground lemon myrtle

2 teaspoons superfine sugar

2 teaspoons rock salt

$\frac{1}{2}$ cup butter, melted

1 cup milk

beaten egg mixed with a little milk, for glazing

whipped cream and jam, to serve

Damper is unleavened bread traditionally made by bushmen and baked in hot ashes—this is a modern version. Bush tucker has become a vital part of Australian culture.

Wattleseed and coffee mini popsicles   **105**

Put the sugar, coffee, and water into a small saucepan and heat slowly until the sugar has dissolved completely, then simmer for 1 minute. Remove from the heat and set aside to cool.

Beat the crème fraîche, wattleseed, and vanilla extract until smooth, then add the cooled sugar syrup and beat again until well combined.

Freeze in an ice-cream maker, following the manufacturer's instructions, until the mixture is thick and slushy. Alternatively, freeze and beat manually (see page 65). Carefully spoon the slushy mixture into two 10-hole ice cube trays, place in the freezer and freeze until the mixture can support sticks in the center, then freeze until firm. (You will have some leftover ice cream, which can be frozen for future use.)

To serve, carefully unmold the mini popsicles and serve immediately.

Makes 20

²/₃ cup granulated sugar

1 tablespoon instant coffee dissolved in
   1 tablespoon warm water

1¼ cups water

1 cup crème fraîche

2 teaspoons ground wattleseed

few drops of vanilla extract

The **wattleseed** is a grain that has been used in cooking by Aborigines for over 6,000 years. Native Australian mint or lemon myrtle can be used instead in this recipe.

106 Barbecued crayfish with chili sauce

First make the chili sauce. Puree the chilies, garlic, ginger, raisins, tomatoes, and vinegar in a food processor or blender. Tip the puree into a saucepan and add the salt, sugar, and water. Bring to a boil, then simmer for 15–20 minutes, until the sauce has thickened slightly. Allow to cool.

Heat a barbecue until the coals are glowing. Arrange the crayfish on a grill rack just above the hot coals and cook for 2–3 minutes on each side. Alternatively, cook the shellfish under a really hot broiler for 5–6 minutes, turning once, until done.

Remove the crayfish from the grill and, holding each one between your finger and thumb, twist off the tail. Hold the tail shell between your thumb and index finger, twist and pull off the flat end—the thread-like intestine will come away. Peel the tail. Discard the rest of the body and shells.

To serve, spoon the sauce into a shallow bowl on a platter and arrange the crayfish tails around it.

Makes 24

24 fresh crayfish (yabbies) or
   jumbo shrimp
lemon wedges, to serve

Sweet chili sauce
5 oz fresh red chilies, seeded
6 garlic cloves
1 teaspoon finely grated fresh
   ginger root
1²/₃ cups golden raisins
7 oz canned tomatoes, drained
white wine vinegar
1 teaspoon salt
1¹/₂ cups superfine sugar
²/₃ cup water

Called **yabbies** in Australia, **crayfish** have a **sweet flavor** and are a **popular addition** to **barbecues**.

Aussie beer-battered fish fingers

Put the flour, salt, pepper, egg, melted butter, and beer in a food processor or blender and process until smooth. Transfer to a large bowl and allow to rest for 30 minutes.

Meanwhile, make the tartare sauce. Combine all the ingredients in a bowl and let stand at room temperature for 15–20 minutes.

Heat the oil in a large, deep saucepan to 375°F. Dip the fish fingers into the batter and fry in batches for 3–4 minutes, or until crisp and golden. Drain each batch on paper towels.

Serve the fish fingers while they are still warm, with the tartare sauce for dipping.

Serves 4–6

1 cup all-purpose flour
1 teaspoon salt
1 teaspoon freshly ground black pepper
1 egg
2 tablespoons butter, melted
²/₃ cup Australian beer
sunflower oil, for deep-frying
1 lb thick white fish fillet (cod or halibut),
    cut into thick fingers

Lemon tartare sauce
1 cup good-quality mayonnaise
thinly grated zest and juice of 1 lemon
2 tablespoons finely chopped capers
1 tablespoon finely chopped red onion
1 teaspoon lemon myrtle salt (optional)
dash of Tabasco sauce

Beer helps to make a very good batter for deep-frying and this combination of fresh fish and a piquant sauce is simple but delicious. Lemon myrtle salt is available from specialty food stores.

110 Coconut chicken in banana leaves

Put the banana leaf squares into a bowl, pour boiling water over them and leave in the water for 3–4 minutes, then drain and set aside.

Cut the chicken into 1½ inch bite-size pieces and put in a large, nonreactive bowl. Mix the coconut cream with the garlic, ginger, coriander, lime zest and juice. Season well with salt and pepper and pour over the chicken. Allow to marinate for 2–3 hours.

Line a two-tier bamboo steamer basket with waxed paper. Remove the chicken from the marinade and wrap each piece in a banana leaf square to cover completely. Secure with toothpicks or skewers. Put the parcels in the steamer baskets and steam over a pan of boiling water for 10–12 minutes, or until just cooked through. Serve warm on the steamer trays, with a bowl for the discarded banana wrappers and toothpicks.

Makes 20

20 banana leaf squares, about
    2½ inches square
2 large, boneless chicken breasts
½ cup coconut cream
2 garlic cloves, crushed
1 teaspoon finely grated fresh
    ginger root
1 teaspoon ground coriander
thinly grated zest and juice of 1 lime
salt and pepper

Steaming in a banana leaf keeps the chicken deliciously tender and it's a popular cooking method throughout the South Pacific. The banana leaves are not edible.

Grilled baby rack of lamb chops

Trim all the excess fat from the lamb racks and, using a sharp knife, cut each rack into 4 small chops. Season well with salt and pepper, put in a shallow bowl, and drizzle with the olive oil. Cover and leave at room temperature for 15–20 minutes.

Combine all the ingredients for the butter in a small bowl. Cover and leave in a cool place until needed.

Arrange the lamb chops in a single layer in a baking dish and broil under a medium-high heat for 4–5 minutes, turning once, or until cooked to your liking. Transfer to a warmed serving platter, spoon a little herb butter over each one and serve immediately.

Makes 20

5 baby racks of New Zealand lamb,
   with 4 chops on each rack
3 tablespoons olive oil
salt and pepper

Rosemary and mint butter
1/2 cup butter, softened
2 tablespoons very finely chopped
   rosemary
2 tablespoons very finely chopped mint

New Zealand is famous for its top-quality lamb, which is best cooked simply to really enjoy its succulent flavor. Here it is enhanced by rosemary and mint butter.

114 Anzac cookies

Line 2 large baking sheets with parchment paper. Mix the oatflakes with the coconut, flour, and sugar in a bowl. Put the butter and corn syrup or molasses in a small bowl and stir over a low heat until they melt. Mix the baking soda with the boiling water and add to the butter mixture, then stir this into the dry ingredients and mix to combine well.

Drop teaspoonfuls of this mixture onto the baking sheets and press lightly with the tines of a fork. Put in a preheated oven, 325°F, for 25–30 minutes, or until golden brown, then remove from the oven and put on wire racks to cool. When cool, arrange the cookies on a platter and serve immediately.

Makes about 48

2½ cups oatflakes

2½ cups unsweetened shredded coconut

2 cups all-purpose flour

1 cup superfine sugar

½ cup butter

1 tablespoon corn syrup or molasses

1 teaspoon baking soda

2 tablespoons boiling water

This was **originally** an army issue cookie that was **essentially** a **substitute for bread**, as it lasted a lot **longer**. Modern varieties are much **more palatable**.

Mini kiwifruit pavlovas **117**

Line a baking sheet, with parchment paper. Put the egg whites in a clean bowl and, using an electric or hand beater, beat until softly peaked. Add the sugar 1 tablespoon at a time, beating well after each addition. Continue to beat until the mixture is thick and glossy, then fold in the vanilla extract.

Using the tips of 2 teaspoons, put 20 walnut-sized spoonfuls onto the baking sheet, spaced well apart, and, with the back of a teaspoon, make an indent in the center of each one. Put in a preheated oven, 350°F, for 5–6 minutes, then reduce the heat to 250°F and bake for 20 minutes until firm. Allow to cool completely, then lift the meringues from the paper.

Whip the cream and sugar until softly peaked. Put the meringues on a serving platter and place a small teaspoon of cream in the center of each one, then top with a couple of slices of kiwifruit. To serve, dust the pavlovas lightly with confectioners' sugar.

Makes 20

2 egg whites

¼ cup superfine sugar

drop of vanilla extract

confectioners' sugar and cocoa powder,
   for dusting

Topping

3 tablespoons heavy cream

1 tablespoon superfine sugar

1 kiwifruit, peeled and sliced

Kiwi seeds were brought to New Zealand from China in the early 1900s. However, it's the flightless bird and not the fruit that's the national symbol of the country.

SOUTH AND CENTRAL AMERICA

120 Spinach and bell pepper quesadillas

Blanch the spinach in a saucepan of boiling water for 1–2 minutes. Drain thoroughly, squeeze out all the excess water and chop finely. Put in a bowl with the bell peppers, garlic, scallions, and cilantro and season well with salt and pepper. In another bowl, mix the mozzarella, Cheddar and sour cream.

Put the tortillas on a clean surface and spread some of the cheese mixture over each one. Carefully spread the spinach mixture over 3 of the prepared tortillas, to come up to the edges of the tortilla. Sandwich this filling with the remaining 3 prepared tortillas, cheese-side down, and press lightly to make 3 stuffed tortilla sandwiches.

Heat a large, nonstick skillet over a medium-high heat and lightly brush with oil. Put a quesadilla in the skillet and, using a spatula, press down lightly while it cooks for 1–2 minutes. Carefully flip it over and cook for 2–3 minutes. Remove and keep warm while you cook the 2 remaining quesadillas. Cut each quesadilla into 8 wedges and serve at once.

Makes 24

8 oz baby spinach leaves

8 oz bottled roasted red bell pepper, drained and finely chopped

1 garlic clove, crushed

4 scallions, very finely chopped

2 tablespoons finely chopped fresh cilantro

10 oz mozzarella cheese, coarsely grated

5 oz Cheddar cheese, coarsely grated

3 tablespoons sour cream

6 x 6 inch flour or corn tortillas

olive oil, for brushing

salt and pepper

Quesadillas are just one variation of the tortilla—a flat bread that is used in many typical Mexican dishes.

Chili and corn muffins with guacamole

Lightly grease two 12-cup mini muffin pans with sunflower oil. Put the flour, cornmeal, baking powder, baking soda, cumin seeds, salt, chilies, cilantro, and sugar in a large bowl. Mix well, then add the egg, buttermilk, and butter and fold together to make a slightly wet batter, adding a little more milk if necessary.

Spoon the batter into the prepared muffin pans and put in a preheated oven, 400°F, for 12–15 minutes, or until risen and golden. Remove from the oven and leave to cool in the pans for 5–10 minutes, before turning out.

Serve the muffins accompanied by bowls of guacamole, sour cream, and salsa.

Makes 24

sunflower oil, for greasing

1 cup all-purpose flour

1/3 cup fine cornmeal

1 teaspoon baking powder

1 teaspoon baking soda

2 teaspoons cumin seeds

large pinch of salt

2 red chilies, seeded and finely chopped

4 tablespoons very finely chopped fresh cilantro

1 tablespoon superfine sugar

1 large egg, beaten

1/2 cup buttermilk

3 tablespoons butter, melted

To serve

guacamole

sour cream

Mexican salsa

When you **eat them**, the **heat from chilies** makes your brain **release endorphins**, so the **more chilies** you have, the **happier you'll feel.**

124 Chorizo, tomato, and onion empanaditas

First make the filling. Heat the oil in a skillet and cook the onion gently for 10 minutes, until lightly browned. Crumble the sausage into the pan. Turn the heat to high and stir-fry for 2–3 minutes, then add the tomato, tomato paste, and stock. Bring to a boil, then reduce the heat, cover the pan and cook gently for 15 minutes, stirring often, until the mixture is thick. Season with salt and pepper and allow to cool.

Line a baking sheet with parchment paper. Roll out the pastry to an ⅛ inch thickness and stamp out 20 circles with a 3 inch round cutter. Put 1 heaped teaspoon of the filling in each circle and fold the pastry into a half-circle. Crimp and seal the edges. Arrange on the baking sheet, brush with egg and put in a preheated oven, 400°F, for 12–15 minutes, or until golden. Serve at once or at room temperature.

Makes 20

12 oz shortcrust pastry
beaten egg, for brushing

Filling
1 tablespoon olive oil
1 large onion, finely chopped
7 oz fresh chorizo sausage, skinned
1 tomato, finely chopped
1 tablespoon tomato paste
½ cup chicken stock
salt and pepper

These little baked turnovers can contain a variety of ingredients and the exact filling is often the specialty of the stallholder.

Red bean, scallion, and rice cakes 127

Mix the rice with the beans and scallions in a bowl, season well with salt and pepper and set aside.

Put the flour, egg, and cream in a bowl, season with salt and pepper and stir to make a smooth batter. Stir in the rice mixture and combine thoroughly.

Brush a large, nonstick skillet with some sunflower oil and place over a medium heat. Working in batches, drop heaped teaspoonfuls of the batter into the hot skillet and cook for 2–3 minutes on each side or until golden and cooked through. Remove each batch to a warmed plate while you cook the rest, brushing the pan with more oil if necessary. Serve immediately with tomato sauce or ketchup for dipping.

Makes about 25

10 tablespoons cooked white rice

5 tablespoons canned red kidney beans,
    drained and roughly chopped

2 scallions, finely sliced

$1/2$ cup all-purpose flour, sifted

1 large egg, beaten

4 tablespoons light cream

sunflower oil, for brushing

salt and pepper

tomato sauce or ketchup, to serve

A good source of protein and iron, beans are a staple part of the Colombian diet, particularly among those communities where meat is scarce.

128 Annatto lamb on red bell pepper boats

Heat the oil in a saucepan and when hot add the annatto seeds, garlic, and lamb. Cook, stirring, over a high heat until the lamb is browned and sealed. Add the oregano, cumin, tomatoes, beer or lager, and bay leaf and bring to a boil. Cover the pan, reduce the heat and cook for 20–25 minutes, or until the mixture is thick and the lamb is tender. Season well with salt and pepper and sprinkle in some chopped cilantro.

Cut each bell pepper into 6 wedges, discarding the stalk and the seeds, to form 18 "boats." To serve, put the red pepper "boats," cut-side up, on a platter and carefully spoon a heaped teaspoonful of the annatto lamb into each. Garnish with fresh cilantro and serve immediately.

Makes 18

1 tablespoon olive oil

1 tablespoon annatto seeds or
   1 teaspoon turmeric

1 garlic clove, crushed

10 oz ground lamb

1 teaspoon dried oregano

1 teaspoon cumin seeds

7 oz canned chopped tomatoes

3 tablespoons beer or lager

1 dried bay leaf, crushed

1 tablespoon chopped fresh cilantro,
   plus extra to garnish

3 large red bell peppers

salt and pepper

Annatto seeds are used extensively in South American cuisine and are often included as much for the orange color they impart as for their flavor. Turmeric can be used instead.

Tuna ceviche and mango phyllo tartlets 131

First make the phyllo shells. Brush the phyllo sheets with melted butter and cut them into 60 x 2½ inch squares. Lightly grease 20 mini muffin holes (2 muffin pans) and line each hole with 3 buttered phyllo squares, placing each one at a slightly different angle, then gently press the phyllo down into the hole to make a tartlet shell. Put in a preheated oven, 350°F, for about 8 minutes until golden and crisp, then remove from the oven, gently take the tartlets out of the pans and leave to cool completely.

Meanwhile, combine all the ingredients for the ceviche in a shallow nonreactive dish, cover and allow to marinate for 10–15 minutes.

To serve, put the phyllo shells on a serving platter and carefully spoon the ceviche into them. Serve the tartlets immediately.

Makes 20

Tartlet shells

7 oz phyllo pastry, thawed if frozen
¼ cup butter, melted

Ceviche

4 oz very, very fresh tuna steak, cut into very fine dice
juice of 1 lemon
2 tablespoons very finely chopped red bell pepper
4 tablespoons finely diced ripe mango flesh
2 tablespoons very finely chopped fresh cilantro
salt to taste

The **origin of ceviche**—raw fish marinated in citrus juice—is a hotly disputed topic, with both Peru and Ecuador claiming the dish as their own.

132 Clams with coconut, lime, and ginger

Scrub the clams and discard any that are open. Heat the oil in a large, nonstick saucepan and add the onion and ginger and cook, stirring, over a medium heat for 6–8 minutes. Stir in the coconut milk, chili, lime zest and juice, and sugar, season well with salt and pepper and bring to a boil. Stir in the cilantro and clams and cook over a medium heat for 5–6 minutes, or until all the clams have opened (discard any that remain closed).

Meanwhile, pour sea salt onto a flat serving platter —this will provide a stable base for the clams.

Remove the clams from the pan with a slotted spoon and discard the top shells. Bring the coconut mixture in the pan to a boil and cook over a high heat until reduced by half. Arrange the clams in their bottom shells on the serving platter and loosen them slightly, to make eating them easier.

Spoon a little coconut sauce over each clam and serve at once. Have finger bowls on hand.

Makes 25

25 fresh, large clams

1 tablespoon sunflower oil

1 onion, very finely chopped

1 inch piece of fresh ginger root, finely chopped

$^3/_4$ cup coconut milk

1 red chili, seeded and finely chopped

juice and thinly grated zest of 2 limes

1 teaspoon superfine sugar

5 tablespoons finely chopped fresh cilantro

sea salt, for lining platter

salt and pepper

Brazilian cuisine has many specific regional variations and specialties and clams are particularly popular on the coast at Salvador de Bahia.

Pumpkin wedges with pebre sauce   **135**

Put all the ingredients for the dipping sauce in a food processor or blender and process until smooth. Transfer to a bowl, cover and leave at room temperature for 2–3 hours to allow the flavors to develop.

Skin and seed the pumpkin, then cut it into 20 bite-size wedges. Put the pieces on a nonstick baking sheet and drizzle with olive oil. Season with salt and put in a preheated oven, 425°F, for 15–20 minutes, or until just tender. Remove the pumpkin from the oven, put it on a platter with the pebre dipping sauce and serve.

Makes 20

½ **medium-size pumpkin**
olive oil, for drizzling
salt

Pebre dipping sauce (Chilean hot sauce)
2 **tablespoons olive oil**
1 **tablespoon white wine vinegar**
6 **tablespoons water**
6 **tablespoons finely chopped fresh cilantro**
1 **small onion, finely chopped**
1 **red chili, seeded and finely chopped**
1 **garlic clove, crushed**
salt to taste

Chile is a **land of contrasts**, not unlike this dish where **sweet** roasted pumpkin is served with a **spicy** dipping sauce.

ARGENTINA

136 Barbecued beef strips

Place the steak between 2 sheets of plastic wrap and, using a wooden mallet or rolling pin, lightly beat to flatten. Remove the plastic wrap and cut the beef into 30 strips about 4 inches long and 1½ inches wide. Arrange the beef strips in a shallow, nonreactive dish in a single layer.

Mix the bay leaves with the peppercorns, red wine, oil, and thyme in a bowl. Pour this over the beef strips and toss to mix well, then cover and marinate in the refrigerator overnight. Soak 30 bamboo skewers in water.

To cook, remove the beef strips from the marinade and thread each one onto a bamboo skewer, then season well with salt and pepper. Position the skewers under a medium-hot broiler or on a barbecue and grill for 4–5 minutes, turning once. Serve beef strips immediately.

Makes 30

1½ lb beef tenderloin steaks
2 dried bay leaves, crushed
10 black peppercorns
1 cup red wine
6 tablespoons light olive or sunflower oil
3–4 sprigs of thyme
salt and pepper

Beef plays an important role in Argentina, both culturally and economically. The asado, or barbecue, is the cooking method of choice.

CARIBBEAN

140 Piña colada ice cream spoons

Put all the ingredients in a food processor or blender and process until thick and smooth. Transfer to an ice-cream machine and freeze according to the manufacturer's instructions. Turn into a shallow freezer container and freeze until ready to serve.

Alternatively, put the ice cream mixture into a shallow freezer container and place it in the freezer for 2–3 hours, or until the sides of the mixture start to set. Remove the ice cream and beat with a fork to break up any ice crystals then return it to the freezer for 2–3 hours. Repeat this process twice more, or until the mixture is smooth and firm.

To serve, using a small melon baller or ice-cream scoop, put small scoops of ice cream onto teaspoons and serve immediately.

Makes 2 cups

½ cup coconut milk
½ cup pineapple juice
¾ cup heavy cream
1 cup confectioners' sugar
2 tablespoons white rum

Rum, the main ingredient in a Piña Colada, was first produced in the Caribbean as a way of using up the by-product of the sugar industry.

Creamy Cuban black bean soup shots **143**

Soak the beans in a large pan of water overnight. Drain and return to the pan. Cover with cold water and boil, uncovered, for 2 hours, or until tender, topping up with boiling water as needed. Drain the beans and set aside.

Heat the oil in a large saucepan and fry the onion for 5–6 minutes until softened. Add the garlic, cumin, oregano, and mustard and stir-fry for 1 minute.

Stir in the stock and the drained beans and bring to a boil. Reduce the heat, cover the pan, and simmer gently for 25–30 minutes. Transfer the soup, in batches, to a food processor or blender and blend until smooth.

To serve, pour the soup into small cups or espresso cups and drizzle a little cream over each one. Sprinkle over some finely diced red bell pepper and serve immediately.

Makes 20 cocktail soup shots

1 cup dried black beans (also known as turtle beans)

1 tablespoon sunflower oil

2 tablespoons finely chopped onion

1 garlic clove, chopped

1 teaspoon ground cumin

1 teaspoon dried oregano

1/4 teaspoon mustard powder

3 cups vegetable stock

light cream, for drizzling

finely diced red bell pepper, to garnish

Black beans provide a link to Cuba's lengthy history, as they were first eaten by the native Indian occupants of the island.

144 Spiced banana and coconut bread

Grease and line an 8 inch square cake pan. Using an electric or hand beater, cream the butter and sugar in a bowl, then stir in the beaten egg.

Sift the flour and baking powder into a separate bowl and add the spices and salt. Stir into the butter mixture alternately with the bananas. Stir in the coconut, then spoon the mixture into the prepared pan.

Put in a preheated oven, 350°F, for 50–60 minutes, or until the bread is firm to the touch and golden. Remove from the oven and stand the bread in the pan on a wire rack for 10 minutes before turning out of the pan, then let cool completely.

To serve, cut into small squares.

Serves 4–6

$\frac{1}{2}$ **cup butter, softened, plus extra**
  for greasing
$\frac{1}{2}$ **cup superfine sugar**
1 egg, lightly beaten
2 cups all-purpose white flour
2 teaspoons baking powder
1 teaspoon ground cinnamon
pinch of grated nutmeg
$\frac{1}{2}$ **teaspoon ground ginger**
$\frac{1}{4}$ **teaspoon salt**
2 ripe bananas, mashed
$\frac{3}{4}$ **cup shredded coconut**

Bananas and sugar are Jamaica's two **biggest exports**; however, **numerous hurricanes** have **threatened** to annihilate banana production over the years.

Chili, sweet potato, and plantain chips

Using a vegetable peeler, cut the sweet potato into very thin, long slices.

Using a sharp knife, peel the plantain and slice it into very thin circles.

Pour the oil into a deep saucepan to one-third full and heat to 350–375°F. Deep-fry the sweet potato and green plantain in batches for 1–2 minutes, or until crisp and golden. Remove each batch with a slotted spoon and drain on paper towels. Sprinkle over the salt and chili powder and serve.

Serves 4–6

1 red sweet potato, peeled
1 green plantain
vegetable oil, for deep-frying
coarse salt, for sprinkling
mild chili powder, for sprinkling

Unlike bananas, plantains must be cooked before being eaten; however, once cooked they can be eaten at every stage of ripeness, from green to dark brown.

148 Fried yam and pineapple sticks

Peel the yam and cut it into 20 bite-size cubes. Peel and core the pineapple and cut it into 20 bite-size cubes.

Heat half the oil in a large nonstick skillet and when hot add the yam cubes, cayenne pepper, and salt. Stir well, then cook over a medium heat for about 10 minutes, or until the yam is lightly browned all over and tender. Remove the yam from the skillet and drain on paper towels.

Wipe the skilet and heat the remaining oil over a high heat. Add the pineapple pieces and stir-fry over a high heat for 2–3 minutes. Remove with a slotted spoon, drain on paper towels and keep warm.

To assemble the sticks, skewer a piece of the fried yam with one of pineapple on a toothpick or small bamboo skewer. Repeat to make 20 sticks and serve immediately.

Makes 20

1½ lb yam
½ ripe, sweet pineapple
6 tablespoons sunflower oil
¼ teaspoon cayenne pepper
salt, to taste

Despite appearances, the yam is not related to the sweet potato. It is a tuber that is grown on vines and there are an astonishing 150 varieties.

Cornmeal and okra squares

Lightly grease 24 nonstick mini muffin holes with sunflower oil. Sift the flour, cornstarch, and baking powder into a bowl and stir in the cornmeal, thyme, garlic salt, cayenne, and oregano. Make a well in the center and pour in the milk and egg. Stir to mix, then pour in the melted butter and fold in gently. Stir in half the sliced okra.

Spoon this batter into the prepared pans and top each one with a couple of slices of the remaining okra. Put in a preheated oven, 350°F, for 20 minutes, or until risen and golden. Remove from the oven and leave to cool in the pans for 10 minutes before turning out.

Serve warm or at room temperature with a tomato salsa, if desired.

Makes 24

sunflower oil, for greasing
1 cup self-rising flour
2 tablespoons cornstarch
$\frac{1}{2}$ teaspoon baking powder
$\frac{1}{2}$ cup fine cornmeal
1 teaspoon dried thyme
2 teaspoons garlic salt
$\frac{1}{2}$ teaspoon cayenne pepper
$\frac{1}{4}$ teaspoon dried oregano
$\frac{3}{4}$ cup milk
1 egg, beaten
2 tablespoons butter, melted
2 okra, very thinly sliced
tomato salsa, to serve (optional)

Okra is native to Africa and it originally found its way to Puerto Rico when slaves brought it with them. It is now an important crop in the country.

152 Papaya, lime, and mango tartlets

Roll out the pastry on a lightly floured surface to an
1/8 inch thickness, then, using a 2 inch round cookie
or pastry cutter, stamp out 20 rounds. Use the
pastry rounds to line 20 x 2 inch mini tartlet pans.
Prick the pastry bases with a fork and line each
tartlet shell with parchment paper and pie weights.
Put in a preheated oven, 400°F, for 10 minutes,
then remove the paper and weights and return the
shells to the oven for 8–10 minutes, or until they
are crisp and golden. Remove from the oven.

Put the lime zest in a blender with the cream and
condensed milk and pulse until well combined. With
the motor running, slowly pour in the lime juice and
process until blended. Transfer to a bowl, cover and
chill in the refrigerator for 3–4 hours, or until firm.

To serve, put the shells on a serving platter and
spoon the lime mixture into each shell. Mix the
mango with the papaya and, using a teaspoon, fill the
shells. Decorate with lime zest and serve immediately.

Makes 20

8 oz sweet shortcrust pastry, thawed
   if frozen
thinly grated zest and juice of 2 large,
   juicy limes
6 tablespoons heavy cream
2/3 cup condensed milk
2 tablespoons finely diced papaya
2 tablespoons finely diced mango
lime zest, to decorate

The **papaya** is quite a **delicate fruit** and is **best stored** in the refrigerator for a **longer life**. Here, the **tangy lime cream contrasts well** with the **sweetness** of the fruit.

Callaloo and Scotch bonnet crostini   **155**

Melt the butter in a large skillet and add the onion and garlic. Cook over a medium heat for 3–4 minutes, then add the thyme and okra and stir-fry over a high heat for 3–4 minutes. Add the spinach and cook for 3–4 minutes until the leaves have wilted.

Stir in the coconut cream and the chili, if using, season with salt and stir-fry over a high heat for 1–2 minutes. Remove from the heat and stir in the crab meat. Toss to mix well and set aside.

Lightly toast the bread rounds on both sides and arrange on a serving platter. Put heaped teaspoonfuls of the callaloo mixture onto the toasted bread and serve immediately.

Makes 20

1 tablespoon butter
1 tablespoon finely chopped onion
1 garlic clove, crushed
1 teaspoon chopped thyme
2 okra, thinly sliced
2$^3/_4$ cups baby spinach leaves
1 tablespoon coconut cream
1 teaspoon finely chopped Scotch bonnet
   chili, seeded (optional)
4 tablespoons fresh white crab meat
20 small rounds of French bread
salt

Callaloo is a traditional soup from the island of Barbados. Here, using the ingredients that go into the soup, are cocktail bites that capture its flavor.

156 Crisp, sweet-spiced twists

Put the flour and salt in a bowl, add the butter and blend with the fingertips until the mixture resembles bread crumbs. Stir in the sugar, cinnamon, caraway seeds, allspice, and orange zest. Stir the egg into the pastry to mix a firm dough.

Turn the dough out onto a lightly floured surface and knead for 4–5 minutes, then roll out to an $\frac{1}{8}$ inch thickness and cut into strips 1 inch wide and 6 inches long. Cut a slit at one end of each strip and pull the other end through it to form a loose "twist." Repeat with the remaining strips to give 20 "twists."

Fill a deep saucepan one-third full with oil and heat to 350°F. Fry the twists, in batches, for 1–1½ minutes, or until golden and crisp. Remove with a slotted spoon and drain on paper towels.

Serve the twists warm or at room temperature, lightly dusted with confectioners' sugar.

Makes 20

1 cup all-purpose flour, sifted
pinch of salt
2 tablespoons butter, chilled and diced
2 tablespoons superfine sugar
1 teaspoon ground cinnamon
2 teaspoons caraway seeds
$\frac{1}{4}$ teaspoon ground allspice
1 teaspoon thinly grated orange zest
1 egg, beaten
sunflower oil, for deep-frying
confectioners' sugar, for dusting

Exotic spices are found all over the **Caribbean**, and are used both in **sweet and spicy dishes**.

160 Canadian wild rice-stuffed mushrooms

Line a baking sheet with parchment paper. Discard the stems of the mushrooms and put the caps on the baking sheet, gill-side up.

Heat the olive oil in a skillet over a medium heat and add the garlic, scallion, and bell pepper. Stir-fry for 4–5 minutes, then add the rice. Cook, stirring, for 1–2 minutes until well combined, then season with salt and pepper and carefully spoon this mixture into the prepared mushroom caps. Sprinkle the cheese over the mushrooms and put in a preheated oven, 400°F, for 10–12 minutes, or until the cheese has melted. Remove the stuffed mushrooms from the oven and serve immediately.

Makes 20

20 large button or chestnut mushrooms, each about 2$\frac{1}{2}$ inches in diameter
1 tablespoon olive oil
2 garlic cloves, finely chopped
1 scallion, finely chopped
1 tablespoon finely diced red bell pepper
$\frac{1}{3}$ cup cooked wild rice
4 oz Monterey Jack or mild Cheddar cheese, finely grated
salt and pepper

Although the name suggests otherwise, wild rice is actually a grain that's native to Canada. Harvesting is strictly controlled and must still conform to traditional methods.

Maple-roast duck rolls

Mix the maple syrup with the soy sauce in a bowl and brush onto the duck breast. Put the duck on a baking sheet and roast in a preheated oven, 400°F, for 15–20 minutes, or until cooked through. Remove from the oven and leave to cool slightly, then, using your fingers, shred the meat into long, thin pieces.

Cut the crêpes or pancakes in half and trim a ¼ inch strip from the rounded edge of each to make 20 straight-sided pieces. Spread some cranberry sauce in the center of each piece, then top with some of the shredded duck and cucumber and scallion strips. Roll the crêpes up tightly and secure each one with a chive tie. Put the rolls on a platter and serve immediately.

Makes 20 rolls

2 teaspoons maple syrup

1 teaspoon soy sauce

1 small duck breast, skinned

10 ready-made thin savory crêpes or pancakes, each about 6 inches in diameter

3 tablespoons cranberry sauce

1 small cucumber, cut into 1½ inch long thin julienne strips

2 scallions, cut into 1½ inch long thin julienne strips

20 long chives, for tying

It was the **Native Americans** who **first discovered** that the **sap** of the maple tree could be **evaporated**, resulting in a sweet, sticky syrup.

164 Quebec apple dumplings

Melt the butter in a nonstick skillet and when it is hot and bubbling, add the apple and sugar. Stir-fry for 2–3 minutes, then add the apple juice, raisins, cinnamon, and allspice. Cook for 1–2 minutes, or until the apple is just tender, then remove from the heat and allow to cool.

Roll out the pastry on a lightly floured surface to an $\frac{1}{8}$ inch thickness. Using a $2\frac{1}{2}$–3 inch round cookie or pastry cutter, stamp out 24 rounds. Brush the edges of the pastry rounds with beaten egg and put a teaspoonful of the apple mixture in the center of each. Fold the rounds in half and, using a fork, press the edges to seal.

Pour the oil into a deep skillet or deep-fat fryer to a depth of at least 3 inches and heat to 375°F. Deep-fry the apple dumplings in batches for 3–4 minutes until well browned. Drain on paper towels and dust liberally with confectioners' sugar before serving.

Makes 24

1 tablespoon butter

1 large apple, peeled, cored, and cut into $\frac{1}{2}$ inch dice

2 teaspoons brown sugar

1 tablespoon apple juice

$\frac{1}{3}$ cup raisins

1 teaspoon ground cinnamon

$\frac{1}{4}$ teaspoon allspice

1 lb sweet shortcrust pastry, thawed if frozen

beaten egg, for brushing

sunflower oil, for deep-frying

confectioners' sugar, for dusting

Apples are the most important fruit crop in Canada and Quebec is one of the main apple-growing areas.

AMERICA

Buttermilk-fried onion rings 167

Put the egg yolks, flour, baking soda, and pinch of salt in a bowl and beat with a large spoon. Gradually pour in the buttermilk, beating until the mixture forms a fairly smooth batter.

Pour the oil into a deep skillet or deep-fat fryer to a depth of at least 3 inches and heat to 375°F.

Separate the onion slices into rings and drop them into the batter. Fry the rings in the hot oil in batches of 7–8, for 4–5 minutes, or until crisp and golden. Drain each batch on paper towels. When all the onion rings are cooked, fry them again in batches in the hot oil for a minute or two to heat them through and crisp them. Drain on paper towels and serve immediately, sprinkled with salt.

Serves 4–6

3 egg yolks
1½ cups all-purpose flour
½ teaspoon baking soda
large pinch of salt, plus salt to sprinkle
1¾ cups buttermilk
sunflower oil, for deep-frying
4 large onions, about 4 inches in diameter, cut into ½ inch slices

Buttermilk was traditionally used so as not to waste the thick liquid that was left after churning the butter.

168 Butterscotch brownies

Base-line an 8 inch square cake pan with parchment paper.

Put the butter and sugar in a saucepan and cook over a low heat, stirring constantly, until the sugar dissolves. Pour this mixture into a bowl and allow to cool until tepid.

Beat the egg and vanilla extract into the butter mixture, then gradually sift in the flour, baking powder, and salt. Gently fold in the walnuts and pour the batter into the prepared cake pan.

Put the cake in the center of a preheated oven, 350°F, for 25–30 minutes, or until it is firm to the touch. Remove it from the oven and let it cool completely in the pan then turn it out and cut into 16 brownies.

Makes 16

¼ cup butter
1 cup dark brown sugar
1 large egg
1 teaspoon vanilla extract
½ cup all-purpose flour
1 teaspoon baking powder
pinch of salt
1 cup walnuts, roughly chopped

The first published recipe for a brownie appeared in the USA in 1897. It is thought the dense, fudgy squares had been made for some time by women who received the recipe by word of mouth.

Cocktail hamburgers

To prepare the buns, make the dough (see first step on page 172). Lightly flour a baking sheet. Knock back the dough, then divide it into 20 pieces. Shape each one into a round ball, place on the baking sheet and press down to form bun shapes. Cover with a cloth and allow to rise for 20 minutes.

Brush the buns with beaten egg and sprinkle with sesame seeds. Bake in a preheated oven, 400°F, for 10–12 minutes. Remove from the oven and cool on a wire rack.

Meanwhile, make the burgers. Line a baking sheet with parchment paper. Mix the beef with the apple, onion, Tabasco, salt, and pepper until well combined. Divide the mixture into 20 portions. Mold each one into a burger shape and place on the baking sheet. Bake for 10–12 minutes.

To serve, split the buns in half and put the burgers on the bottom halves. Top each burger with ketchup, onion rings, and tomatoes. Put the tops on and secure with toothpicks.

Makes 20

Burger buns
2 cups white bread flour, sifted
pinch of salt
²⁄₃ cup hand-warm water
2 teaspoons olive oil
1 heaping teaspoon easy-blend
   dried yeast
beaten egg, for brushing
sesame seeds, for sprinkling
tomato ketchup
small onion rings
sliced cherry tomatoes

Burgers
8 oz lean ground beef
1 tablespoon finely chopped apple
1 tablespoon finely chopped onion
dash of Tabasco sauce
salt and pepper

The first **hamburger** chain was started in 1916 in **Kansas**, but it took a **few more years** before the idea really **took hold** in America.

172 New York-style hot dogs

First make the hot dog buns. Put the flour in a bowl with the salt, make a well in the center and add the water and oil. Sprinkle the dried yeast over the liquid and leave for 2–3 minutes to dissolve. Gently draw in the flour from the sides of the bowl and knead to a sticky dough. Turn the dough out on a floured surface and knead for 10 minutes until elastic and smooth. Place in a bowl, cover with plastic wrap, and allow to rise in a warm place for 1½ hours.

Lightly flour a baking sheet. Knock back the dough, divide it into 20 portions and shape each one into a cylinder, about 1¼ inches long. Put on the baking sheet, cover, and allow to rise for 20 minutes.

Brush each roll with egg and put in a preheated oven, 400°F, for 10–12 minutes, or until lightly browned and cooked through. Remove from the oven and cool on a wire rack.

To serve, split each roll lengthwise along the top. Fill with a cocktail frankfurter or sausage. Pipe over the mustard and ketchup and serve.

Makes 20

20 mini cocktail frankfurters or
  sausages
American-style mustard
tomato ketchup

Hot dog buns
2 cups white bread flour, sifted
pinch of salt
²/₃ cup hand-warm water
2 teaspoons olive oil
**1 heaping teaspoon easy-blend
  dried yeast**
beaten egg, for brushing

The **hot dog** stand is a **quintessential** New York institution and one that has been **feeding hungry passers-by** since the late 1800s.

Lobster and tarragon puffs   **175**

Line a large baking sheet with parchment paper.
Roll out the pastry on a lightly floured surface to a
¼ inch thickness. Using a 2½ inch round cookie or
pastry cutter, stamp out 40 rounds. Put 20 of the
rounds on the baking sheet, spaced well apart, and
brush with beaten egg. Using a 1¼ inch cutter,
stamp out circles from the center of the remaining
rounds. Discard the inner pastry circles, leaving you
with 20 pastry "rings." Put these "rings" on the
brushed pastry rounds and gently press to seal.
Brush again with the beaten egg, then put in a
preheated oven, 400°F, for 12–15 minutes, or until
risen and golden. Remove from the oven and put on
a wire rack to cool completely.

Meanwhile, make the filling. Put the lobster meat
in a bowl and mix in the mayonnaise, mustard, bell
pepper and tarragon. Season well with salt and
pepper and, using a teaspoon, carefully spoon into
the cold puff shells. Garnish with sprigs of tarragon
and serve immediately.

Makes 20

Puff shells
7 oz puff pastry, thawed if frozen
beaten egg, for glazing

Filling
5 oz lobster tail meat, chopped into
 ½ inch dice
4 tablespoons mayonnaise
1 teaspoon American-style mustard
1 tablespoon very finely diced red bell
 pepper
2 tablespoons very finely chopped
 tarragon
salt and pepper
tarragon sprigs, to garnish

Lobster wasn't always considered a luxury: when the
colonists first settled in New England they thought them a pest
and used the meat as fish bait.

176 Blueberry griddle cakes

Sift the flour, baking powder, sugar, and salt into a large bowl. Make a well in the center and pour in the eggs and milk. Using a large spoon, mix just long enough for the mixture to blend, then stir in the butter and blueberries. Don't overmix: the griddle cakes will be lighter if the batter is not too smooth.

Heat a griddle pan or a heavy skillet over a moderate heat until a drop of water flicked onto it evaporates immediately. Lightly grease the pan with a pastry brush dipped in sunflower oil. Using a small ladle, pour in enough batter to form a pancake 2–2½ inches in diameter. Cook for 2–3 minutes until small bubbles form, then flip the pancake over and cook for 1 minute on the other side until lightly browned. Repeat, using up the batter and lightly greasing the pan as required.

Serve the griddle cakes on a warmed platter, with drizzled maple syrup and a bowl of whipped cream.

Makes 30–35

2 cups all-purpose flour

2 teaspoons baking powder

2 teaspoons superfine sugar

large pinch of salt

3 eggs, lightly beaten

1¾ cups milk

¼ cup butter, melted

⅔ cup fresh blueberries

sunflower oil, for greasing

maple syrup and whipped cream,
   to serve

The **blueberry** is **indigenous** to North America. Before the **Pilgrim Fathers** arrived, **Native Americans** were enjoying these **juicy berries** all year round, thanks to **clever** preservation techniques.

California sushi cones

Bring the rice and water to a boil in a pan over a medium heat. Cover tightly, reduce the heat to very low and cook for about 15 minutes, or until the rice is tender. Remove from the heat and allow to stand, covered, for 10–15 minutes.

Put the vinegar and sugar in a small saucepan and cook over a medium heat until the sugar dissolves. Remove from the heat and allow to cool. Spoon the sushi rice onto a platter and drizzle over the vinegar mixture. Sprinkle with the sesame seeds and toss gently. Cover with a damp cloth. Allow to cool.

Cut the nori sheets into 40 x 2½ inch squares and place shiny side down. Divide the rice mixture into 40 and spread one portion in an even layer over the left half of each nori square. Spread a little wasabi over the rice and top with an avocado slice, a cucumber strip, a mushroom, and a kari slice. Roll the nori squares into little cones starting at the left corner. Moisten the edges with a wet finger and extra rice to seal them. Repeat to make 40 cones. Serve immediately with a dipping sauce.

Makes 40

¾ cup Japanese sushi rice

1 cup water

½ cup rice vinegar

4 tablespoons superfine sugar

2 tablespoons roasted sesame seeds

7–8 sheets of nori

2 teaspoons prepared wasabi or hot mustard

2 Haas avocados, peeled, pitted, and cut into 40 long slices

1 cucumber, seeded and cut into 40 x 2 inch julienne strips

40 enoki mushrooms

40 slices kari (pickled ginger)

tamari or soy sauce, to serve

Despite being **sushi**, the **California cone** did, in fact, **originate** in California as a **response** to the Western **reticence** toward **eating raw fish**.

180 Chili-bean burritos

Roughly crush the beans and put in a bowl with the onion, cumin, cilantro, chili, and oregano.

Lay the tortillas out on a clean surface and spread 1½ tablespoons of the bean mixture on one half of each tortilla. Roll once to enclose the filling, tuck both ends toward the center and continue to roll—the burritos should now be 3½–4 inches long.

Arrange the burritos in a single layer on a nonstick baking sheet, seam-side down, and sprinkle the Cheddar over them. Cover loosely with foil and put in a preheated oven, 350°F, for 6–8 minutes, then remove the foil and bake for a further 3–4 minutes, or until they are warmed through. Remove the burritos from the oven, cut in half, sprinkle with paprika and serve immediately.

Makes 30

13 oz canned red kidney beans, drained
1 red onion, finely chopped
1 teaspoon ground cumin
3 tablespoons finely chopped fresh
   cilantro
1 red chili, seeded and finely chopped
1 tablespoon finely chopped oregano
15 small flour tortillas
2 oz Cheddar cheese, finely grated

Chilies and corn form the backbone of this fusion cuisine whose popularity has spread around the globe.

Mini Key lime pies

To make the lime filling, pour the lime juice into a bowl and beat in the zest, egg yolks, and sugar. Pour into a saucepan and cook over a low heat for 2 minutes, stirring, or until the sugar has dissolved. Gradually add the butter, stirring, and cook for about 10 minutes until thick and glossy. Remove from the heat, cover the surface with plastic wrap to prevent a skin from forming and chill until needed.

Lay the pastry on a lightly floured surface and, using a 2½ inch round cookie or pastry cutter, cut out 48 rounds and use to line 48 x 1½ inch tartlet or mini pie pans. Line each with parchment paper and pie weights. Put in a preheated oven, 350°F, for 8–10 minutes, then remove the paper and weights and return to the oven for 6–8 minutes, or until crisp and golden. Remove from the oven and leave to cool in the pans.

To serve, spoon a little of the lime filling into each pastry shell, dust with confectioners' sugar and decorate with candied lime zest, if using.

Makes 48

⅔ cup lime juice

thinly grated zest of 4 limes

6 egg yolks

½ cup superfine sugar

½ cup chilled butter, diced

4 sheets ready-rolled shortcrust
  pastry, about 10 inches square,
  thawed if frozen

confectioners' sugar, for dusting

candied lime zest, to decorate (optional)

Key limes are smaller than **Persian limes** and yellow in color. Introduced to the **Florida Keys** by early **Spanish settlers**, the fruit **flourished** and **adopted the name** of its new home.

184 Double chocolate meringue whispers

Line a baking sheet with parchment paper. Put the egg whites in a clean bowl and beat until softly peaked. Add the sugar 1 tablespoon at a time, beating well after each addition. Continue to beat until the mixture is thick and glossy, then fold in the cocoa powder and mint extract until just combined.

Fit a piping bag with a large star nozzle, fill with the meringue mixture and pipe 40 rosettes 1¼ inches apart on the baking sheet. Put in a preheated oven, 250°F, for about 1 hour, or until crisp and dry. Allow to cool completely before removing from the parchment paper.

Put the chocolate in a small bowl and melt over a pan of simmering water, then allow to cool. Whip the cream until softly peaked.

Hold each meringue rosette by its point and dip its base into the melted chocolate. Sandwich 2 of the prepared rosettes with 1 teaspoon of whipped cream and repeat to make 20 "whispers". Arrange them on a plate and dust lightly with cocoa powder.

Makes 20

2 egg whites
½ cup superfine sugar
1 teaspoon cocoa powder, sifted
drop of mint extract
4 oz bittersweet chocolate
½ cup whipping cream
cocoa powder, for dusting

Milton Hershey, founder of America's most famous chocolate company, began trading in his home state of Pennsylvania in around 1875.

GLOSSARY

Annatto seed: Small, indented, pyramid-shaped seed of the annatto tree, with a powdery, red-oxide-like covering. The flavor is mild, somewhat peppery and earthy.

Enoki mushroom: A delicate mushroom that grows in clumps of spaghetti-like strands, each with a small, snow-white cap.

Foie gras: Liver, usually from force-fed geese.

Kaffir lime leaf: Glossy, dark green, aromatic leaf, available fresh or dried.

Kirsch: Brandy distilled from cherries.

Lebanese cucumber: Smaller and crunchier than an ordinary cucumber.

Lemon myrtle: Leaves of the lemon tea tree.

Long bean: Also known as yard-long bean, because of its size. Similar to, but more pliable than, a green bean.

Nori: Japanese name for a blade-like red seaweed. Usually sold as a rectangular sheet, it is the most commonly eaten alga in Japan.

Plantain: A tropical fruit similar to a banana, but larger and with green skin.

Scotch bonnet chili: A small, hot chili named from its resemblance to a Scottish hat.

Sushi rice: Short-grained rice.

Tahini: A thick paste made from ground sesame seeds.

Tamari: Similar to, but thicker than, soy sauce, tamari is a dark sauce made from soy beans.

Wasabi: Japanese version of horseradish, from the root of an Asian plant. Available as ready-made sauce or in powdered form.

Wattleseed: From the Australian wattle tree, the seeds have a coffee/chocolate/hazelnut flavor and are dark brown.

INDEX

188

Africa 57–79
almonds: crisp almond
and sesame samsa
61
Greek phyllo and nut
baklavas 55
annatto lamb on red bell
pepper boats 128
Antigua 152
Anzac cookies 114
apple dumplings, Quebec
164
Argentina 136
Asia 81–99
Aussie beer-battered fish
fingers 109
Australasia 101–17
Australia 102–9
Austria 38
avocados: California
sushi cones 179
chili and corn muffins
with guacamole 123

Bahamas 140
baklavas, Greek phyllo
and nut 55
banana and coconut
bread 144
banana leaves, coconut
chicken in 110
Barbados 155
bean curd: gado gado
97
beans: chili-bean
burritos 180

red bean, scallion, and
rice cakes 127
beef: barbecued beef
strips 136
beefsteak tartare on
endive scoops 26
chili beef and lime
lettuce wraps 90
cocktail hamburgers
171
maschi canapés 69
mini beef goulash and
gherkin pies 41
mini bobotie open pies
78
beer: Aussie beer-
battered fish fingers
109
broiled mussels with
herbed beer butter
30
zucchini flower fritters
45
Belgium 30
bell peppers: annatto
lamb on red bell pepper
boats 128
goats' cheese and red
bell pepper puffs 22
spinach and bell pepper
quesadilla wedges
120
black bean soup shots
143
blinis with sour cream
and caviar 42

blueberry griddle cakes
176
bobotie open pies
78
Brazil 132
bread: callaloo and
Scotch bonnet
crostini 155
damper squares with
lemon myrtle 102
lab with toasted flat-
bread dippers 70
seared foie gras on
French bread 33
smoked salmon and
gubbeen bites 21
spiced banana and
coconut bread 144
brownies, butterscotch
168
buns 171, 172
burgers: cocktail
hamburgers 171
burritos, chili-bean 180
buttermilk-fried onion
rings 167
butterscotch brownies
168

California sushi cones
179
callaloo and Scotch
bonnet crostini 155
Canada 160–5
Canadian wild rice-stuffed
mushrooms 160

Caribbean 139–57
caviar, blinis with sour
cream and 42
cheese: chili-bean
burritos 180
goats' cheese and red
bell pepper puffs 22
lab with toasted flat-
bread dippers 70
Manchego and
membrillo bites 49
Pecorino shortbread
rounds with pesto 53
Raclette fondue with
baby potato dippers
37
Reblochon, tomato, and
ham quichettes 34
rye, chive, and cream
cheese squares 17
smoked salmon and
gubbeen bites 21
spinach and pepper
quesadilla wedges
120
steamed Chinese
purses 86
chicken: coconut chicken
in banana leaves 110
mini quail Scotch eggs
18
piri-pri chicken
drumettes 77
Chile 135
chili: barbecued crayfish
with chili sauce 106

callaloo and Scotch
bonnet crostini 155
chili and corn muffins
with guacamole 123
chili-bean burritos 180
chili beef and lime
lettuce wraps 90
chili crab on mini
noodle nests 94
chili, sweet potato, and
plantain chips 147
oyster Mombasa 73
piri-piri chicken
drumettes 77
salt and chili squid 89
China 86–9
Chinese purses, steamed
86
chips, chili, sweet potato,
and plantain 147
chocolate meringue
whispers 184
chorizo, tomato, and
onion empanaditas 124
cilantro: pumpkin wedges
with pebre sauce
135
clams with coconut, lime,
and ginger 132
cocktail hamburgers 171
cocktail Spice Island fish
cakes 74
coconut: Anzac cookies
114
coconut chicken in
banana leaves 110

spiced banana and
coconut bread 144
coconut milk: clams with
coconut, lime, and
ginger 132
piña colada ice cream
spoons 140
cod: Aussie beer-battered
fish fingers 109
coffee: wattleseed and
coffee mini ice creams
105
Colombia 127
cookies, Anzac 114
cornmeal: chili and corn
muffins 123
cornmeal and okra
squares 151
couscous: lemon and
couscous-stuffed
tomatoes 58
crab: callaloo and Scotch
bonnet crostini
155
chili crab on mini
noodle nests 94
crayfish with chili sauce
106
Cuba 143
cucumber: California
sushi cones 179
herring and dill-
cucumber skewers 14
maple-roast duck rolls
163
maschi canapés 69

damper squares with
lemon myrtle 102
Denmark 17
dips 62, 85, 97
Dominican Republic 148
duck rolls, roast 163
dumplings, Quebec apple
164

Ecuador 128
eggplant dip with
crudités 62
eggs: green pea, potato,
and mint tortilla bites
49
mini quail Scotch eggs
18
Egypt 62
empanaditas, chorizo,
tomato, and onion 124
endive scoops, beefsteak
tartare on 26
England 25
Ethiopia 70
Europe 13–55

fish cakes, cocktail Spice
Island 74
fish fingers, Aussie beer-
battered 109
foie gras on French
bread 33
fondue, Raclette 37
France 33–5
French fries 25
fritters 45, 85, 167

gado gado 97
Germany 26
goats' cheese and red
bell pepper puffs 22
Greece 55
Greek phyllo and nut
baklavas 55
griddle cakes, blueberry
176
guacamole, chili and
corn muffins with 123

Haiti 147
halibut: cocktail Spice
Island fish cakes 74
ham: mini
schinkenfleckerln 38
prosciutto and scallop
spiedini 46
Reblochon, tomato, and
ham quichettes 34
hamburgers, cocktail 171
herring and dill-cucumber
skewers 14
Holland 29
hot dogs, New York-style
172
Hungary 41

ice cream: peanut ice
cream in phyllo shells
65
piña colada ice cream
spoons 140
wattleseed and coffee
popsicles 105

190

India 82–5
Indonesia 97
Ireland 21
Italy 45–7

Jamaica 144
Japan 98

Kenya 73
Key lime pies 183
kiwifruit pavlovas 117

lab with toasted flat-
  bread dippers 70
lamb: annatto lamb on
  red bell pepper boats
  128
  grilled baby rack of
  lamb chops 113
lettuce wraps, chili beef
  and lime 90
Liberia 66
lime: chili beef and lime
  lettuce wraps 90
  mini Key lime pies 183
  papaya, lime, and
  mango tartlets 152
lobster and tarragon
  puffs 175

Manchego and
  membrillo bites 49
mangoes: papaya, lime,
  and mango tartlets
  152
  tuna ceviche and

mango phyllo tartlets
  131
maple-roast duck rolls
  163
maschi canapés 69
meatballs: rosemary and
  veal frikadeller skewers
  29
meringues: double
  chocolate meringue
  whispers 184
  mini kiwifruit pavlovas
  117
Mexico 120–3
Morocco 58
Mozambique 77
muffins, chili and corn
  123
mushrooms: California
  sushi cones 179
  Canadian wild rice-
  stuffed mushrooms
  160
mussels with herbed
  beer butter 30

New York-style hot dogs
  172
New Zealand 113–17
noodles: chili crab on
  mini noodle nests 94
mini schinkenfleckerin
  38
soba, tobiko, and
  scallion spoons 98
nori: California sushi

cones 179
North America 159–85

oatflakes: Anzac cookies
  114
okra: cornmeal and okra
  squares 151
onions: buttermilk-fried
  onion rings 167
  onion and gram flour
  fritters 85
oyster Mombasa 73

papaya, lime, and
  mango tartlets 152
pastries: chorizo, tomato,
  and onion
  empanaditas 124
  crisp almond and
  sesame samsa 61
  goats' cheese and red
  bell pepper puffs 22
  Greek phyllo and nut
  baklavas 55
  lobster and tarragon
  puffs 175
  spicy pea and potato
  samosas 82
  see also pies; tartlets
pavlovas, mini kiwifruit
  117
peanut ice cream in
  phyllo shells 65
peas: green pea, potato,
  and mint tortilla
  bites 49

spicy pea and potato
  samosas 82
Pecorino shortbread
  rounds with pesto 53
Peru 131
pesto, Pecorino
  shortbread rounds with
  53
pies: mini beef goulash
  and gherkin pies 41
  mini bobotie open pies
  78
  see also pastries
piña colada ice cream
  spoons 140
pineapple: fried yam and
  pineapple sticks 148
  piña colada ice cream
  spoons 140
piri-piri chicken drumettes
  77
potatoes: cocktail Spice
  Island fish cakes 74
  crispy whitebait and
  French fry cones 25
  green pea, potato, and
  mint tortilla bites 49
  Raclette fondue with
  baby potato dippers
  37
  rosemary and veal
  frikadeller skewers 29
  spicy pea and potato
  samosas 82
prosciutto and scallop
  spiedini 46

Puerto Rico 151
pumpkin wedges with
    pebre sauce 135

quail Scotch eggs 18
Quebec apple dumplings
    164
quesadilla wedges,
    spinach and bell pepper
    120

Raclette fondue with
    baby potato dippers 37
Reblochon, tomato, and
    ham quichettes 34
red kidney beans:
    chili-bean burritos
    180
    red bean, scallion,
    and rice cakes 127
rice: California sushi
    cones 179
    maschi canapés 69
    red bean, scallion,
    and rice cakes 127
rosemary and veal
    frikadeller skewers 29
rum: piña colada ice
    cream spoons 140
Russia 42
rye, chive, and cream
    cheese squares 17

salt and chili squid 89
Samoa 110
samosas, spicy pea and

potato 82
Sardinia 53
sausages: New York-style
    hot dogs 172
scallops: prosciutto and
    scallop spiedini 46
schinkenfleckerin, mini
    38
Scotch eggs, mini quail
    10
Scotland 18
Senegal 65
shortbread rounds,
    Pecorino 53
shrimp: fragrant shrimp
    and herb rolls 93
    steamed Chinese
    purses 86
Sicily 46
Singapore 94
smoked salmon and
    gubbeen bites 21
soba, tobiko, and scallion
    spoons 98
soup shots, creamy
    Cuban black bean 143
South Africa 78
South America 119–37
Spain 49–51
spinach: callaloo and
    Scotch bonnet
    crostini 155
    spinach and bell pepper
    quesadilla wedges
    120
squid, salt and chili 89

Sudan 69
sushi cones, California
    179
Sweden 14
sweet potatoes: chili,
    sweet potato and
    plantain chips 147
    sweet potato pone 66
Switzerland 37

tartlets: mini Key lime
    pies 103
    papaya, lime, and
    mango tartlets 152
    Reblochon, tomato, and
    ham quichettes 34
    tuna ceviche and
    mango phyllo tartlets
    131
Thailand 90
tomatoes: lemon and
    couscous-stuffed
    tomatoes 58
    Reblochon, tomato, and
    ham quichettes 34
tortillas: chili-bean
    burritos 180
    green pea, potato,
    and mint tortilla bites
    49
    spinach and bell pepper
    quesadilla wedges
    120
Trinidad 156
tuna ceviche and mango
    phyllo tartlets 131

Tunisia 61
twists, crisp, sweet-
    spiced 156

United States of
    America 167–85

veal: rosemary and veal
    frikadeller skewers 29
vegetables: gado gado 97
    smoky eggplant dip
    with crudités 62
Venezuela 124
Vietnam 93

Wales 22
walnuts: butterscotch
    brownies 168
    Greek phyllo and nut
    baklavas 55
wattleseed and coffee
    mini popsicles 105
whitebait and French fry
    cones 25
wild rice-stuffed
    mushrooms 160
wonton wrappers:
    steamed Chinese
    purses 86

yam and pineapple sticks
    148

Zanzibar 74
zucchini flower
    fritters 45

ACKNOWLEDGMENTS

192

Executive Editor Sarah Ford

Editor Jessica Cowie

Executive Art Editor Geoff Fennell

Designer Janis Utton

Photographer Stephen Conroy

Food Styling Sunil Vijayakar

Styling Liz Hippisley

Picture Research Jennifer Veall

Senior Production Controller Martin Croshaw

Picture Acknowledgments

Special Photography © Octopus Publishing Group Limited
/Stephen Conroy

Other Photography:

Alamy/Sue Cunningham Photographic 133; /Robert
Harding Picture Library Ltd. 20; /Gavin Hellier 16;
/David Norton Photography 92; /RogerPix 44

Corbis UK Ltd/Patrick Bennett 165; /Barnabas Bosshart
68; /Jan Butchofsky-Houser 22; /David Cumming;
Eye Ubiquitous 145; /Ric Ergenbright 27; /Owen
Franken 48; /Stephen Frink 150; /Paul Hardy 39;
/Jon Hicks 11; /Robert van der Hilst 122; /Jeremy
Horner 142; /Kit Houghton 137; /Rob Howard 71;
/Mark A. Johnson 79; /Wolfgang Kaehler 7;
/Bob Krist 170; /David Lees 52; /Jean-Pierre
Lescourret 32; /Michael S. Lewis 161; /Ludovic
Maisant 149; /Lance Nelson 103; /Charles O'Rear 96;
/M L Sinibaldi 54, 178; /Pablo Corral Vega 129, 134;
/Patrick Ward 60; /Alison Wright 157

Eye Ubiquitous/Liz Barry 28; /James Davis Travel
Photography 82; /Julia Waterlow 63

Getty Images/Jerry Driendl 185

Caroline Jones/108, 115, 166

Panos/Mark Henley 86; /Marc Schlossman 76